Thematic Oral Language

Grade 3

How To Use

The lesson for each day should take no more than five or ten minutes to complete. It is important that these exercises become a part of the daily class routine.

Option #1
Write the incorrect sentences on the board. Have the students copy the incorrect sentences on paper and make the necessary corrections using a red pencil. Then work together as a class. As errors are identified orally by the students, correct the sentences on the board. Make sure students explain the reason for each correction. Underline any error(s) not found by the students. Then give the students an opportunity to state the reason for the error(s). Students may then copy the corrected sentences on their paper.

Option #2
Write the incorrect sentences on the board. After the children have read each sentence silently, have them indicate the errors orally, giving the reason for each correction. Correct the sentences on the board.

Option #3
Make copies of the pages of incorrect sentences, cut in half, and hand out to students at the beginning of each week. Children can make their corrections on the paper using a red pencil. The corrections should be discussed in class.

Format

The daily lessons are set in a two-page format of three columns. The first column contains the incorrect sentences. The second column shows the same sentences with corrections. The third column lists the skills covered within the sentences.

Guidelines for Skills Addressed

- The comma helps to make written language clear. **Thematic Oral Language** uses a comma after each item in a series. If your textbook makes the last comma optional, you may wish to complement your instruction by deleting the final series comma we have used.

- Special nouns such as mother, dad, and aunt are capitalized only when they are not preceded by a possessive word or other determiner.
    I gave Dad a book.
    I gave my dad a book.

- The need for an exclamation point is not always obvious. It may be necessary for you to read the sentence aloud to assist students in the decision.

- The abbreviations A.M. and P.M. can be written in upper or lower case. Since most texts use upper case, **Thematic Oral Language** has followed this rule.

- The term *Article* (Art.) rather than *Determiner* is used for *a, an* and *the*.

- The term *Demonstrative adjective* (Dem. adj.) is used for the pronominal demonstrative adjectives *this, that, these* and *those*. Use the term(s) with which your students are familiar.

- There is a difference of opinion on the capitalization of the words *earth, moon,* and *sun*. Follow the rule you are most comfortable with. **Thematic Oral Language** will follow the rule which says to capitalize only when personifying or when using with the names of other bodies of the solar system.

- An apostrophe after a number (e.g. 1900's) is optional. We have chosen to use the apostrophe in these instances. Likewise, periods are optional with the abbreviation for miles per hour (m.p.h.).

- Underlining is used in place of italics whenever appropriate.

- Teachers are encouraged to incorporate additional skills wherever they deem appropriate.

Note: **Capitalization of the pronoun *I*, capital letters at the beginning of a sentence, and periods at the end of declarative or imperative sentences are not listed under the "skills covered" section due to their common and frequent use. For the First Grade book these guidelines take effect after the first few weeks.**

Abbreviations Used in *Skills Covered* Column

This is a generic list of abbreviations compiled for all grade levels of **Thematic Oral Language**. Certain skills may not be addressed in the book you are using. Appearance and space were taken into consideration when deciding whether or not to use an abbreviation.

Abbreviation – Abbr.
Adjective – Adj.
Adverb – Adv.
Apostrophe – Apostro.
Appositive – Appos.
Article – Art.
Capitalize – Cap.
Comma(s) – Com.
Compound sentence – Comp. sent.
Conjunction – Conj.
Contraction – Contr.
Demonstrative adjective – Dem. adj.
Direct address – Dir. addr.
Direct quotation – Dir. quot.
Double negative – Dbl. neg.
Double subject – Dbl. subj.
Enunciation – Enunc.
Exclamation point – Excl. pt.
First word of direct quotation – 1st word of dir. quot.
First word after interjection – 1st word after interj.
First word of split quotation – 1st word split quot.
Geographic feature – Geo. fea.
Geographic location – Geo. loc.
Government – Gov.
Group – Gr.

Homonym(s) – Hom.
Improper – Improp.
Improper usage – Improp. use.
Irregular plural – Irreg. pl.
Interjection – Interj.
Introductory phrase – Intro. phrase
Month – Mo.
Nationality – Nation.
Noun – N.
Number – Num.
Object – Obj.
Period – Per.
Person(s) – Pers.
Possessive – Poss.
Pronoun – Pron.
Proper – Prop.
Question mark – Ques. mark
Quotation marks – Quot. marks
Relative/Relationship – Rel.
Run-on sentence – Run-on
Singular – Sing.
Split quotation – Split quot.
Subject – verb agreement – Subj.–v. agree.
Underline – Under.
Verb – V.

©1993 Instructional Fair, Inc.   IF8403 Oral Language

Week 1 – Mountain Animals

Day		
1	Language Arts	a. theres a animal from the rabbit family called the american pika but it looks more like a guinea pig b. what do pikas eat if they live so high in the mountains asked mark
2	Science	a. the snow leopards summer home is as far up as 13000 feet in the mountains of central asia b. isnt the snow leopard six or more feet long i asked
3	Social Studies	a. mountain lions live mainly in british columbia california and new mexico but some live in florida b. isnt the mountain lion also known as an cougar puma or panther
4	Math	a. male bighorn sheep stand about three too four feet tall and weigh 200 to 300 pounds reported charles b. bighorns they live in the highest parts of mountains and they often live in groups of 50 too 60
5	Creative Arts	a. didnt phil take a picture of them sheep for national geographic magazine b. he selled some of his pictures of deer mountain lions and goats to a magazine called ranger rick

Week 2 – Grassland Animals

Day		
1	Language Arts	a. did dad learn you that a hippopotamus lives in the lakes rivers and ponds of the african grasslands b. its really surprising to i that they eat fruit grass leaves and vegetables
2	Science	a. a baby kangaroo is called an joey and it is about won inch long when its born b. the joey leaves its mothers pouch after six months but it returns when theres danger
3	Social Studies	a. do ostriches live on the plains and deserts of africa asked jeff b. there was ostrich farms in africa the united states and australia in the early 1900s
4	Math	a. karen didnt knowed there was a african elephant named jumbo that stood eleven feet tall b. her goed to the fifth street library and read that its weight was more than 14000 pounds
5	Creative Arts	a. my uncle jim are a animal sculptor and him collect figures of african animals b. mrs lucas she teached us how two form lions out of clay last tuesday

©1993 Instructional Fair, Inc.   IF8403 Oral Language

Corrected Sentences  Skills Covered

1	There's an animal from the rabbit family called the American pika, but it looks more like a guinea pig.	Apostro. (contr.), Art. (an); Cap. (prop. adj. – country); Com. (before **but** in comp. sent.)
	"What do pikas eat if they live so high in the mountains?" asked Mark.	Quot. marks (dir. quot.); Ques. mark (dir. quot.); Cap. (prop. n. – person)
2	The snow leopard's summer home is as far up as 13,000 feet in the mountains of central Asia.	Apostro. (poss.); Com. (num.); Cap. (prop. n. – continent)
	"Isn't the snow leopard six or more feet long?" I asked.	Quot. marks (dir. quot.); Apostro. (contr.); Ques. mark (dir. quot.)
3	Mountain lions live mainly in British Columbia, California, and New Mexico, but some live in Florida.	Cap. (prop. n. – province, states); Com. (series, before **but** in comp. sentence)
	Isn't the mountain lion also known as a cougar, puma, or panther?	Apostro. (contr.); Art. (a); Com. (series); Ques. mark
4	"Male bighorn sheep stand about three to four feet tall and weigh 200 to 300 pounds," reported Charles.	Quot. marks (dir. quot.); Homonym (to); Com. (dir. quot.); Cap. (prop. n. – person)
	Bighorns live in the highest parts of the mountains, and they often live in groups of 50 to 60.	Dbl. subj.; Com. (before **and** in comp. sentence); Homonym (to)
5	Didn't Phil take a picture of those sheep for <u>National Geographic</u> magazine?	Apostro. (contr.); Cap. (prop. n. – person, magazine); Dem. adj.; Underline (magazine); Ques. mark
	He sold some of his pictures of deer, mountain lions, and goats to a magazine called <u>Ranger Rick</u>.	Verb; Com. (series); Cap. (prop. n. – magazine); Underline (magazine)

1	Did Dad teach you that a hippopotamus lives in the lakes, rivers, and ponds of the African grasslands?	Cap. (prop. n. – relationship, prop. adj. – continent); Improp. usage (teach); Com. (series); Ques. mark
	It's really surprising to me that they eat fruit, grass, leaves, and vegetables.	Apostro. (contr.); Pron. (case); Com. (series)
2	A baby kangaroo is called a joey, and it is about one inch long when it's born.	Art. (a); Com. (before **and** in comp. sentence); Homonym (one); Apostro. (contr.)
	The joey leaves its mother's pouch after six months, but it returns when there's danger.	Apostro. (poss., contr.); Com. (before **but** in compound sentence)
3	"Do ostriches live on the plains and deserts of Africa?" asked Jeff.	Quot. marks (dir. quot.); Cap. (prop. n. – continent, person); Ques. mark (dir. quot.)
	There were ostrich farms in Africa, the United States, and Australia in the early 1900's.	Subj. – v. agree.; Cap. (prop. n. – continents, country); Com. (series); Optional apostro. (date)
4	Karen didn't know there was an African elephant named Jumbo that stood eleven feet tall.	Cap. (prop. n. – person, pet; prop. adj. – nationality); Apostro. (contr.); Verb; Art. (an);
	She went to the Fifth Street Library and read that its weight was more than 14,000 pounds.	Pron. (case); Verb; Cap. (prop. n. – institution); Com. (number)
5	My Uncle Jim is an animal sculptor, and he collects figures of African animals.	Cap. (prop. n. – title, person; prop. adj. – continent); Subj. – v. agree.; Art. (an); Com. (before **and** in comp. sentence); Pronoun (case)
	Mrs. Lucas taught us how to form lions out of clay last Tuesday.	Cap. (prop. n. – title, person, day); Period (abbr.); Dbl. subj.; Verb; Homonym (to)

©1993 Instructional Fair, Inc.   IF8403 Oral Language

Week 3 – Forest Animals

Day			
1	Language Arts	a.	chucks book report was about rain forests and cloud forests the book written by michael emsley
		b.	sue and amy told us class about a article about parrots in the ranger rick magazine
2	Science	a.	kerry said miss french told us that monkeys squirrels and parrots live in trees
		b.	me and larry didnt know that some lizards frogs and snakes live their, to
3	Social Studies	a.	moose they are called elk everywhere except in north america said the guide in yellowstone national park
		b.	dont us found moose mainly in canada and alaska
4	Math	a.	maria read that a dear can runned 30 miles per hour but a moose can run only 20 mph
		b.	she brother jose was surprised that a elephant and a rabbit can both run about 20 mph
5	Creative Arts	a.	our teacher ms porter asked us to brang cardboard boxes colored paper and yarn to class on wednesday
		b.	were gonna surprise everyone by making leopards tigers and bears for the art show in december

Week 4 – Desert Animals

Day			
1	Language Arts	a.	did you knew that the word "mouse" come from an old sanskrit word that means "thief"
		b.	mice they lives all over the world, even in desert areas
2	Science	a.	us discovered that grasshopper mice likes to eat grasshoppers scorpions worms and insects
		b.	the grasshopper mouse it probably got its name because it like to eat grasshoppers
3	Social Studies	a.	aunt wilma seen grasshopper mice as her drived threw the desert in arizona
		b.	arent grasshopper mice finded in mexico, to
4	Math	a.	a camel it stand 6 to 7 feet tall at the shoulders said jesse
		b.	jordan and me heard that an camel usually carries 400 pounds but they can carry up to 1000 pounds
5	Creative Arts	a.	mrs grants class painted rocks with pictures of bobcats coyotes and jack rabbits on them
		b.	use the narrow brush to paint the cats whiskers cautioned mrs grant

©1993 Instructional Fair, Inc.   IF8403 Oral Language

Corrected Sentences

Skills Covered

1	✓ Chuck's book report was about <u>Rain Forests and Cloud Forests</u>, the book written by Michael Emsley.	Cap. (prop. n. – persons, book); Apostro. (poss.); Underline (book); Com. (appos.)
	Sue and Amy told our class about an article about parrots in the <u>Ranger Rick</u> magazine.	Cap. (prop. n. – persons, magazine); Verb; Pronoun (case); Art. (an); Underline (magazine)
2	✓ Kerry said, "Miss French told us that monkeys, squirrels, and parrots live in trees."	Cap. (prop. n. – persons, title); Com. (dir. quot., series); Quot. marks (dir. quot.); Verb
	Larry and I didn't know that some lizards, frogs and snakes live there, too.	Cap. (prop. n. – person); Pron. (order, case); Apostro. (contr.); Com. (series); Homonyms (there, too)
3	"Moose are called elk everywhere except in North America," said the guide in Yellowstone National Park.	Quot. marks (dir. quot.); Dbl. subj.; Cap. (prop. n. – continent, park); Com. (dir. quot.)
	Don't we find moose mainly in Canada and Alaska?	Apostro. (contr.); Pronoun (case); Verb; Cap. (prop. n. – country, state); Ques. mark
4	Maria read that a deer can run 30 miles per hour, but a moose can run only 20 m.p.h.	Cap. (prop. n. – person); Homonym (deer); Verb; Com. (before **but** in comp. sent.); Optional periods (abbr.)
	Her brother, Jose, was surprised that an elephant and a rabbit can both run about 20 m.p.h.	Pron. (case); Com. (appos.); Cap. (prop. n. – person); Art. (an); Optional periods (abbr.)
5	Our teacher, Ms. Porter, asked us to bring cardboard boxes, colored paper, and yarn to class on Wednesday.	Com. (appos., series); Cap. (prop. n. – title, person, day); Period (abbr.); Verb
	We're going to surprise everyne by making leopards, tigers, and bears for the art show in December.	Apostro. (contr.); Enunciation (going to); Com. (series); Cap. (prop. n. – month)

1	Did you know that the word "mouse" comes from an old Sanskrit word that means "thief"?	Verb; Subj. – v. agree.; Cap. (prop. adj. – language); Ques. mark
	Mice live all over the world, even in desert areas.	Double subject; Subj. – v. agreement
2	We discovered that grasshopper mice like to eat grasshoppers, scorpions, worms, and insects.	Pron. (case); Subj. – v. agree.; Com. (series)
	The grasshopper mouse probably got its name because it likes to eat grasshoppers.	Double subject; Subj. – v. agree.
3	Aunt Wilma saw grasshopper mice as she drove through the desert in Arizona.	Cap. (prop. n. – title, person, state); Verbs; Pron. (case); Hom. (through)
	Aren't grasshopper mice found in Mexico, too?	Apostro. (contr.); Verb; Cap. (prop. n. – country); Homonym (too); Ques. mark
4	"A camel stands 6 to 7 feet tall at the shoulders," said Jesse.	Quot. marks (dir. quot.); Dbl. subj.; Subj. – v. agree.; Com. (dir. quot.); Cap. (prop. n.– person)
	Jordan and I heard that a camel usually carries 400 pounds, but they can carry up to 1,000 pounds.	Cap. (prop. n. – person); Pron. (case); Art. (a); Com. (before **but** in comp. sent., number)
5	Mrs. Grant's class painted rocks with pictures of bobcats, coyotes, and jack rabbits on them.	Cap. (prop. n. – title, person); Period (abbr.); Apostro. (poss.); Com. (series)
	"Use the narrow brush to paint the cat's whiskers," cautioned Mrs. Grant.	Quot. marks (dir. quot.); Apostro. (poss.); Com. (dir. quot.); Cap. (prop. n. – title, person); Period (abbr.)

©1993 Instructional Fair, Inc.   IF8403 Oral Language

Week 5 – Polar Animals

Day			
1	Language Arts	a.	the magazine called international life contained a article about arctic animals in its march-april issue
		b.	didnt you read a article about the north and south poles in a magazine kids discover
2	Science	a.	why do the snowy owls of the north pole molt there brown summer down in september
		b.	thats so theyll be white and blend into the arctic snow answered uncle phillip
3	Social Studies	a.	i new that bears walruses snowy owls and musk oxen lived in the arctic regions of asia canada and europe
		b.	i couldnt believe that their was arctic bumblebees living there, to
4	Math	a.	a adult polar bear are about 9 feet long and it can way more than 1000 pounds
		b.	polar bears they have won or too cubs at a time and each cubs weight is about one pound at birth
5	Creative Arts	a.	mrs hart our art teacher had us make clay polar bears and then she displayed them the hole month of may
		b.	didnt she takes sum of them to the oak street art show in may, to

Week 6 – Ocean Animals

Day			
1	Language Arts	a.	i read a article about many strange-sounding fish in the february-march issue of national wildlife
		b.	did mr banch read the living sea by jacques cousteau
2	Science	a.	a lionfishs fins have sharp spines that are filled with poison said dr t m brown
		b.	is it dangerous too people i asked
3	Social Studies	a.	the decline of sperm whaling in america begined with the california gold rush in 1849
		b.	the us government halted all commercial whaling in the united states in 1971
4	Math	a.	isnt it amazing that the stingrays in the waters near australia can be fourteen foots long
		b.	me and tom thinks its amazing that some flying fish can fly up to 1000 feet
5	Creative Arts	a.	three of cousteaus films about the sea has one academy awards
		b.	their are beautiful paintings of sea life in a book by james fisher wonderful world of the sea

©1993 Instructional Fair, Inc.   IF8403 Oral Language

Corrected Sentences  Skills Covered

1	The magazine called <u>International Life</u> contained an article about Arctic animals in its March-April issue.	Cap. (prop. n. – magazine; prop. adj. – region, months); Underline (magazine); Art. (an)
	Didn't you read an article about the North and South Poles in a magazine, <u>Kids Discover</u>?	Apostro. (contr.); Art. (an); Cap. (prop. n. – places, magazine); Com. (appos.); Underline (magazine); Ques. mark
2	Why do the snowy owls of the North Pole molt their brown summer down in September?	Cap. (prop. n. – place, month); Homonym (their); Ques. mark
	"That's so they'll be white and blend into the Arctic snow," answered Uncle Phillip.	Quot. marks (dir. quot.); Apostro. (contr.); Cap. (prop. adj. – region; prop. n. – title, person); Com. (dir. quot.)
3	I knew that bears, walruses, snowy owls, and musk oxen lived in the Arctic regions of Asia, Canada, and Europe.	Homonym (knew); Com. (series); Cap. (prop. adj. – region; prop. n. – continents, country)
	I couldn't believe that there were Arctic bumblebees living there, too.	Apostro. (contr.); Homonyms (there, too); Subj. – v. agree.; Cap. (prop. adj. – region)
4	An adult polar bear is about 9 feet long, and it can weigh more than 1,000 pounds.	Art. (an); Subj. – v. agree.; Com. (before **and** in comp. sent., number); Homonym (weigh)
	Polar bears have one or two cubs at a time, and each cub's weight is about one pound at birth.	Dbl. subj.; Homonyms (one, two); Com. (before **and** in comp. sent., poss.); Apostro. (poss.)
5	Mrs. Hart, our art teacher, had us make clay polar bears, and then she displayed them the whole month of May.	Cap. (prop. n. – title, person, month); Period (abbr.); Com. (appos., before **and** in comp. sent.); Homonym (whole)
	Didn't she take some of them to the Oak Street Art Show in May, too?	Apostro. (contr.); Verb; Homonyms (some, too); Cap. (prop. n. – event, month); Ques. mark

1	I read an article about many strange-sounding fish in the February-March issue of <u>National Wildlife</u>.	Art. (an); Cap. (prop. adj. – months; prop. n. – magazine); Under. (magazine)
	Did Mr. Branch read the book <u>The Living Sea</u> by Jacques Cousteau?	Cap. (prop. n. – title, persons, book); Period (abbr.); Under. (book); Ques. mark
2	"A lionfish's fins have sharp spines that are filled with poison," said Dr. T.M. Brown.	Quot. marks (dir. quot.); Apostro. (poss.); Com. (dir. quot.); Cap. (prop. n. – title, person); Periods (abbr.)
	"Is it dangerous to people?" I asked.	Quot. mark (dir. quot.); Homonym (to); Ques. mark (dir. quot.)
3	The decline of sperm whaling in America began with the California gold rush in 1849.	Cap. (prop. n. – country, state); Verb
	The U.S. government halted all commercial whaling in the United States in 1971.	Cap. (prop. adj. – nationality; prop. n. – country); Periods (abbr.)
4	Isn't it amazing that the stingrays in the waters near Australia can be fourteen feet long?	Apostro. (contr.); Cap. (prop. n. – continent); Irreg. plural (feet); Ques. mark
	Tom and I think it's amazing that some flying fish can fly up to 1,000 feet.	Cap. (prop. n. – person); Pron. (case, order); Subj. – v. agree.; Apostro. (contr.); Com. (number)
5	Three of Cousteau's films about the sea have won Academy Awards.	Cap. (prop. n. – person, award); Apostro. (poss.); Subj. – v. agree.; Homonym (won)
	There are beautiful paintings of sea life in a book by James Fisher, <u>Wonderful World of the Sea</u>.	Homonym (there); Cap. (prop. n. – person, book); Underline (book); Com. (appos.)

Week 7 – Poetry

Day		
1	Language Arts	a. mrs richards gived my little sister an book of nursery rhymes called mother goose b. her gave it to her in september four she forth birthday
2	Science	a. too of glorias favorite poems by jack prelutsky are my brothers bug and my snake b. the book of a thousand poems gots lotsa poems about creatures seasons and flowers said mrs willis
3	Social Studies	a. unhappy south pole penguin a poem about penguins are randys favorite poem b. im gonna look for poems about famous americans and don said that theyre in a book in our library
4	Math	a. eighteen flavors a poem by shel silverstein mentions sum of mine favorite kinds of ice cream, to b. nursery rhymes they have learned us the days of the week months of the year and how two count
5	Creative Arts	a. lets has a storybook character parade in october instead of a halloween parade b. doug and karen was gonna paint an picture of little boy blue on the walls of hill preschool

Week 8 – Folk Stories

Day		
1	Language Arts	a. ms andrews said did you no that folk literature includes fairy tales folk tales fables ballads and epics b. won of mine favorite folk tale books are talking drums of africa by christine price
2	Science	a. werent myths often created to answer questions about nature i asked dr martin b. he sayed that people they maked up stories about gods and heroes who controlled natural forces
3	Social Studies	a. why mosquitoes buzz in peoples ears are a book based on a african folk tale b. didnt verna aardema writed that book
4	Math	a. mine teacher asked us if us knowed what fairy tail book tells about a girl with seven little friends b. pam and sue was the only to people who new it were snow white and the seven dwarfs
5	Creative Arts	a. we seen the opera hansel and gretel at the grant concert hall in december b. we thinked the story comed from a german folk tale gathered by jakob and wilhelm grimm

©1993 Instructional Fair, Inc.   IF8403 Oral Language

Corrected Sentences   Skills Covered

1	Mrs. Richards gave my little sister a book of nursery rhymes called <u>Mother Goose</u>.	Cap. (prop. n. – title, person, book); Period (abbr.); Verb; Art. (a); Underline (book)
	She gave it to her in September for her fourth birthday.	Pron. (cases); Cap. (prop. n. – month); Homonyms (for, fourth)
2	Two of Gloria's favorite poems by Jack Prelutsky are "My Brother's Bug" and "My Snake."	Hom. (two); Cap. (prop. n. – persons, poems); Apostro. (poss.); Quot. marks (poems)
	"<u>The Book of a Thousand Poems</u> has lots of poems about creatures, seasons, and flowers," said Mrs. Willis.	Quot. marks (dir. quot.); Cap. (prop. n. – book, title, person); Under. (book); Verb; Enunc. (lots of); Com. (series, dir. quot.); Period (abbr.)
3	"Unhappy South Pole Penguin," a poem about penguins, is Randy's favorite poem.	Cap. (prop. n. – poem, person); Quot. marks (poem); Com. (appos.); Subj. – verb agree. Apostro. (poss.)
	I'm going to look for poems about famous Americans, and Don said that they're in a book in our library.	Apostro. (contr.); Enunciation (going to); Cap. (prop. n. – nationality, person); Com. (before **and** in comp. sent.)
4	"Eighteen Flavors," a poem by Shel Silverstein, mentions some of my favorite kinds of ice cream, too.	Quot. marks (title); Cap. (prop. n. – poem, person); Com. (appos.); Hom. (some, too); Pron. (case)
	Nursery rhymes have taught us the days of the week, months of the year, and how to count.	Dbl. subj.; Improp. usage (teach); Com. (series); Homonym (to)
5	Let's have a storybook character parade in October instead of a Halloween parade.	Apostro. (contr.); Subj. – v. agree.; Cap. (prop. n. – month, holiday)
	Doug and Karen were going to paint a picture of Little Boy Blue on the walls of Hill Preschool.	Cap. (prop. n. – persons, character, institution); Subj. – v. agree.; Enunciation (going to); Article (a)

1	Ms. Andrews said, "Did you know that folk literature includes fairy tales, folk tales, fables, ballads, and epics?"	Cap. (prop. n. – title, person, 1st word dir. quot.); Period (abbr.); Com. (dir. quot., series); Quot. marks (dir. quot.); Hom. (know); Ques. mark
	One of my favorite folk tale books is <u>Talking Drums of Africa</u> by Christine Price.	Homonym (one); Pron. (case); Subj. – v. agree.; Cap. (prop. n. – book, person); Underline (book)
2	"Weren't myths often created to answer questions about nature?" I asked Dr. Martin.	Quot. marks (dir. quot.); Apostro. (contr.); Ques. mark (dir. quot.); Cap. (prop. n. – title, person); Period (abbr.)
	He said that people made up stories of gods and heroes who controlled natural forces.	Verbs; Double subject
3	<u>Why Mosquitoes Buzz in People's Ears</u> is a book based on an African folk tale.	Cap. (prop. n. – book; prop. adj. – continent); Apostro. (poss.); Underline (book); Subj. – v. agree.; Art. (an)
	Didn't Verna Aardema write that book?	Apostro. (contr.); Cap. – (prop. noun – person); Verb; Ques. mark
4	My teacher asked us if we knew what fairy tale book tells about a girl with seven little friends.	Pron. (case); Verb; Homonym (tale)
	Pam and Sue were the only two people who knew it was <u>Snow White and the Seven Dwarfs</u>.	Cap. (prop. n. – persons, book); Subj. – v. agree.; Homonyms (two, knew); Underline (book)
5	We saw the opera "Hansel and Gretel" at the Grant Concert Hall in December.	Verb; Quot. marks (title); Cap. (prop. n. – opera, building, month)
	We thought the story came from a German folk tale gathered by Jakob and Wilhelm Grimm.	Verbs; Cap. (prop. adj. – nationality; prop. n. – persons)

Week 9 – Fiction

Day		
1	Language Arts	a. childrens fiction it includes stories about adventure fantasy and animals said mr kelly b. ive herd that judy blume is an famous american author born in elizabeth new jersey
2	Science	a. billy said ive always wondered how mary poppins flyed over london england b. theres a very funny picture of an spaceship in the book miss pickerell goes to mars
3	Social Studies	a. didnt you read little navajo bluebird a story about a navajo girl b. i readed it and i also read the book strawberry girl, which takes place in rural florida in the early 1900s
4	Math	a. louisa may alcott she writed a story about for sisters growing up in new england b. ann said mine favorite book is ramona quimby, age 8 a story about a girl in third grade
5	Creative Arts	a. wont the students at van creative arts school perform a play next march called charlottes web b. steve tony and angie they wanta paint the scenery on saturday at 200 pm

Week 10 – Biographies

Day		
1	Language Arts	a. there is some great books about famous people in the drake library on elm street said mr thomas pike b. whats the difference between a biography and a autobiography asked curtis
2	Science	a. a weed is a flower: the life of george washington carver was wrote and illustrated by aliki b. the story of ben franklin was wrote by eve merriam and it tells about the famous inventors life
3	Social Studies	a. rosa parks a book wrote by eloise greenfield was illustrated by eric marlow b. its the story of a woman whose arrest beginned a bus strike in montgomery alabama
4	Math	a. ten brave women tell about the lives of susan b anthony and nine other women b. john f kennedy a biography is about the life of the 35th president of the united states
5	Creative Arts	a. tobi tobias he writed maria tallchief a biography about an famous ballerina b. isnt trumpeters tale: the story of young louis armstrong about a famous jazz musician

Corrected Sentences  Skills Covered

1	"Children's fiction includes stories about adventure, fantasy, and animals," said Mr. Kelly.	Quot. marks (dir. quot.); Apostro. (poss.); Dbl. subj.; Com. (series, dir. quot.); Cap. (prop. n. – title, person); Period (abbr.)
	I've heard that Judy Blume is a famous American author born in Elizabeth, New Jersey.	Apostro. (contr.); Homonym (heard); Cap. (prop. n. – person, city, state; prop. adj. – nationality); Com. (city, state)
2	Billy said, "I've always wondered how Mary Poppins flew over London, England."	Cap. (prop. n. – person; 1st word in quot.; character, city, country); Com. (dir. quot., city, country); Quot. marks (dir. quot.); Apostro. (contr.); Verb
	There's a very funny picture of a spaceship in the book <u>Miss Pickerell Goes to Mars</u>.	Apostro. (contr.); Art. (a); Cap. (prop. n. – book); Underline (book)
3	Didn't you read <u>Little Navajo Bluebird</u>, a story about a Navajo girl?	Apostro. (contr.); Cap. (prop. n. – book; prop. adj. – tribe); Underline (book); Com. (appos.); Ques. mark
	I read it, and I also read the book <u>Strawberry Girl</u>, which takes place in rural Florida in the early 1900's.	Verb; Com. (before **and** in comp. sent.); Cap. (prop. n. – book, state); Underline (book); Optional apostro. (date)
4	Louisa May Alcott wrote a story about four sisters growing up in New England.	Cap. (prop. n. – person, geo. location); Dbl. subj.; Verb; Homonym (four)
	Ann said, "My favorite book is <u>Ramona Quimby, Age 8</u>, a story about a girl in third grade."	Cap. (prop. n. – person, book, 1st word in quot.); Com. (dir. quot. appos.); Quot. marks (dir. quot.); Pronoun (case); Underline (book);
5	Won't the students at Van Creative Arts School perform a play next March called <u>Charlotte's Web</u>?	Apostro. (contr., poss.); Cap. (prop. n. – institution, month, play); Underline (play); Ques. mark
	Steve, Tony, and Angie want to paint the scenery on Saturday at 2:00 P.M.	Cap. (prop. n. – persons, day, optional abbr.); Com. (series); Dbl. subj.; Enunciation (want to); Colon (time); Periods (abbr.)

1	"There are some great books about famous people in the Drake Library on Elm Street," said Mr. Thomas Pike.	Quot. marks (dir. quot.); Subj. – v. agree.; Cap. (prop. n. – institution, street, title, person); Com. (dir. quot.); Period (abbr.)
	"What's the difference between a biography and an autobiography?" asked Curtis.	Quot. marks (dir. quot.); Apostro. (contr.); Art. (an); Ques. mark (dir. quot); Cap. (prop. n. – person)
2	<u>A Weed Is a Flower: The Life of George Washington Carver</u> was written and illustrated by Aliki.	Cap. (prop. n. – book, person); Underline (book); Verb
	<u>The Story of Ben Franklin</u> was written by Eve Merriam, and it tells about the famous inventor's life.	Cap. (prop. n. – book, person); Underline (book); Verb; Com. (before **and** in comp. sent.); Apostro. (poss.)
3	<u>Rosa Parks</u>, a book written by Eloise Greenfield, was illustrated by Eric Marlow.	Cap. (prop. n. – book, persons); Com. (appos.); Under. (book); Verb
	It's the story of a woman whose arrest began a bus strike in Montgomery, Alabama.	Apostro. (contr.); Verb; Cap. (prop. n. – city, state); Com. (city, state)
4	<u>Ten Brave Women</u> tells about the lives of Susan B. Anthony and nine other women.	Cap. (prop. n. – book, person); Underline (book); Subj. – v. agree.; Period (abbr.)
	<u>John F. Kennedy</u>, a biography, is about the life of the 35th President of the United States.	Cap. (prop. n. – book, title, country); Underline (book); Period (abbr.); Com. (appos.)
5	Tobi Tobias wrote <u>Maria Tallchief</u>, a biography about a famous ballerina.	Cap. (prop. n. – person, book); Dbl. subj.; Verb; Com. (appos.); Art. (a); Underline (book)
	Isn't <u>Trumpeter's Tale: The Story of Young Louis Armstrong</u> about a famous jazz musician?	Apostro. (contr.; poss.); Cap. (prop. n. – book); Underline (book); Ques. mark

©1993 Instructional Fair, Inc.   IF8403 Oral Language

Week 11 – Information Books

Day		
1	Language Arts	a. information books is nonfiction books that tell about science history and sports said mrs bates b. david asked his grandma mary to buy mysteries and marvels of ocean life a book by rick morris
2	Science	a. paws hoofs and flippers is a book wrote and illustrated by olive l earle b. roma gans wrote a book about the molting habits of birds and its titled when birds change their features
3	Social Studies	a. the book called lets find out about the united nations was wrote by martha and charles shapp b. roberto he were looking four an book about hospitals and medicine at the yankee clipper library
4	Math	a. there is 111 american folk songs and ballads in a book folk song, u s a wrote by john a lomax b. an book about math was wrote by irving and ruth adler and it was called sets and numbers for the very young
5	Creative Arts	a. paint all kinds of pictures is a book that tells how to use paper paint and brushes said mrs kingsberry b. donald myrus writed about all kinds of music in a book ballads blues and the big beat

Week 12 – Magazines

Day		
1	Language Arts	a. when i had to stay home from stoneybrook school last friday i readed kids discover my favorite magazine b. isnt my weekly reader used in many schools in the united states
2	Science	a. ranger rick magazine has many good articles about dolphins bears birds and insects said josh and paul b. does the magazine 3-2-1 contact has articles about science nature and technology
3	Social Studies	a. there was a article in ebony magazine in january about martin luther king jr b. boys life was started by the boy scouts in 1911 and american girl was began by the girl scouts in 1917
4	Math	a. cant you get ten issues of that magazine four $15.95 a year asked grandma olive b. humpty dumpty magazine is for young children but ranger rick are written for ages 6 –12
5	Creative Arts	a. i like the beautiful photographs in national geographic my favorite magazine said stanley b. roger said i agree but i like the pictures in ranger rick and kids discover, to

©1993 Instructional Fair, Inc.   14   IF8403 Oral Language

Corrected Sentences  Skills Covered

	Corrected Sentences	Skills Covered
1	"Information books are nonfiction books that tell about science, history, and sports," said Mrs. Bates.	Quot. marks (dir. quot.); Subj. – v. agree.; Com. (series, dir. quot.); Cap. (prop. n. – title, person); Period (abbr.)
	David asked his Grandma Mary to buy <u>Mysteries and Marvels of Ocean Life</u>, a book by Rick Morris.	Cap. (prop. n. – persons, title, book); Underline (book); Com. (appos.)
2	<u>Paws, Hoofs, and Flippers</u> is a book written and illustrated by Olive L. Earle.	Cap. (prop. n. – book, person); Com. (series); Underline (book); Verb; Period (abbr.)
	Roma Gans wrote a book about the molting habits of birds, and it's titled <u>When Birds Change Their Features</u>.	Cap. (prop. n. – person, book); Com. (before **and** in comp. sent.); Apostro. (contr.); Under. (book)
3	The book called <u>Let's Find Out About the United Nations</u> was written by Martha and Charles Shapp.	Cap. (prop. n. – book, persons); Under. (book); Apostro. (contr.); Verb
	Roberto was looking for a book about hospitals and medicine at the Yankee Clipper Library.	Cap. (prop. n. – person, institution); Dbl. subj.; Subj. – v. agree.; Homonym (for); Art. (a)
4	There are 111 American folk songs and ballads in a book, <u>Folk Song, U.S.A.</u>, written by John A. Lomax.	Subj. – v. agree.; Cap. (prop. adj. – nationality; prop. n. – book, person); Under. (book); Com. (appos.); Periods (abbr.); Verb
	A book about math was written by Irving and Ruth Adler, and it was called <u>Sets and Numbers for the Very Young</u>.	Art. (a); Verb; Cap. (prop. n. – persons, book); Com. (before **and** in comp. sent.); Under. (book)
5	"<u>Paint All Kinds of Pictures</u> is a book that tells how to use paper, paint, and brushes," said Mrs. Kingsberry.	Quot. marks (dir. quot.); Cap. (prop. n. – book, title, person); Under. (book); Com. (series, dir. quot.); Period (abbr.)
	Donald Myrus wrote about all kinds of music in a book, <u>Ballads, Blues, and the Big Beat</u>.	Cap. (prop. n. – person, book); Verb; Com. (appos., series); Under. (book)

1	When I had to stay home from Stoneybrook School last Friday, I read <u>Kids Discover</u>, my favorite magazine.	Cap. (prop. n. – institution, day, magazine); Verb; Underline (magazine); Com. (intro. clause, appos.)
	Isn't <u>My Weekly Reader</u> used in many schools in the United States?	Apostro. (contr.); Cap. (magazine, country); Under. (magazine); Ques. mark
2	"<u>Ranger Rick</u> magazine has many good articles about dolphins, bears, birds, and insects," said Josh and Paul.	Quot. marks (dir. quot.); Cap. (prop. n. – magazine, persons); Underline (magazine); Com. (series, dir. quot.)
	Does the magazine <u>3-2-1 Contact</u> have articles about science, nature, and technology?	Cap. (prop. n. – magazine); Under. (magazine); Subj. – v. agree.; Com. (series); Ques. mark
3	There was an article in <u>Ebony</u> magazine in January about Martin Luther King, Jr.	Art. (an); Cap. (prop. n. – magazine, person, title, month); Under. (magazine); Optional Com. (before title); Period (abbr.)
	<u>Boy's Life</u> was started by the Boy Scouts in 1911, and <u>American Girl</u> was begun by the Girl Scouts in 1917.	Cap. (prop. n. – magazines, organizations); Apostro. (poss.); Under. (magazines); Com. (before **and** in a comp. sent.); Verb
4	"Can't you get ten issues of that magazine for $15.95 a year?" asked Grandma Olive.	Quot. marks (dir. quot.); Apostro. (contr.); Homonym (for); Ques. mark (dir. quot.); Cap. (prop. n. – title, person)
	<u>Humpty Dumpty Magazine</u> is for young children, but <u>Ranger Rick</u> is written for ages 6–12.	Cap. (prop. n. – magazines); Under. (magazines); Com. (before **but** in comp. sent.); Subj. – v. agree.
5	"I like the beautiful photographs in <u>National Geographic</u>, my favorite magazine," said Stanley.	Quot. marks (dir. quot.); Cap. (prop. n. – magazine, person); Under. (magazine); Com. (appos., dir. quot.)
	Roger said, "I agree, but I like the pictures in <u>Ranger Rick</u> and <u>Kids Discover</u>, too."	Cap. (prop. n. – person, first word in quot., magazines); Com. (dir. quot.; before **but** in comp. sent.); Quot. marks (dir. quot.); Under. (magazines); Hom. (too)

Week 13 – Pioneer Transportation

Day			
1	Language Arts	a.	suzanne hilton she wrote a book about pioneer travel called getting there: frontier travel without power
		b.	wasnt the conestoga wagon first used buy american pioneers traveling over the allegheny mountains
2	Science	a.	when a conestoga wagons wheels were removed the wagon it could be strapped to a raft and floated across a river
		b.	why couldnt it float with its wheels on asked andrea
3	Social Studies	a.	freight lines was needed two carry mail gold and other supplies from san francisco to new york city
		b.	did henry wells and william g fargo they began the wells, fargo & company in 1852
4	Math	a.	wagon trains goed about won oar too miles per hour and it took about seven days to went 100 miles
		b.	an stagecoach went won hundred miles in 24 ours but it had to travel day and night
5	Creative Arts	a.	stagecoaches covered wagons and a train is included in an mural showing the pioneers means of travel
		b.	we went to the grand rapids art museum and we gotted to sit in a covered wagon said nick

Week 14 – Pioneer Trails

Day			
1	Language Arts	a.	the oregon trail a book by francis parkman helped ms freemans class learned about pioneer travel
		b.	didnt the discovery of the cumberland gap make travel across the appalachian mountains easier
2	Science	a.	the cumberland gap is narrow and its sides are about five hundred feet high said dr march
		b.	the pioneers they didnt has power tools so they had to use axes hammers and hoes to do there work
3	Social Studies	a.	independence missouri was the start of the oregon trail and this trail helped expand the united states
		b.	the sante fe trail also beginned in independence missouri but it ended in santa fe new mexico
4	Math	a.	wasnt the oregon trail 2000 miles long asked naomi
		b.	the trip it taked about six months in a covered wagon and many people died on the trail
5	Creative Arts	a.	whats on ms clarks list of things we need four our play about pioneers traveling west on the trails
		b.	we all thinked us needed a spinning wheel a iron kettle and a babys cradle

©1993 Instructional Fair, Inc. IF8403 Oral Language

Corrected Sentences  Skills Covered

1	Suzanne Hilton wrote a book about pioneer travel called <u>Getting There: Frontier Travel Without Power</u>.	Cap. (prop. n. – person, book); Dbl. subj.; Underline (book)
	Wasn't the Conestoga wagon first used by American pioneers traveling over the Allegheny Mountains?	Apostro. (contr.), Cap. (prop. adj. – thing, nationality; prop. n. – geographic feature); Homonym (by); Ques. mark
2	When a Conestoga wagon's wheels were removed, the wagon could be strapped to a raft and floated across a river.	Cap. (prop. adj. – thing); Apostro. (poss.); Com. (intro. clause); Dbl. subj.
	"Why couldn't it float with its wheels on?" asked Andrea.	Quot. marks (dir. quot.); Apostro. (contr.); Ques. mark (dir. quot.); Cap. (prop. n. – person)
3	Freight lines were needed to carry mail, gold, and other supplies from San Francisco to New York City.	Subj. – v. agree.; Homonym (to); Com. (series), Cap. (prop. n. – cities)
	Did Henry Wells and William G. Fargo begin the Wells, Fargo & Company in 1852?	Cap. (prop. n. – persons, business); Period (abbr.); Dbl. subj.; Verb; Com. (series); Ques. mark
4	Wagon trains went about one or two miles per hour, and it took about seven days to go 100 miles.	Verbs; Homonyms (one, or, two); Com. (before **and** in comp. sentence)
	A stagecoach went one hundred miles in 24 hours, but it had to travel day and night.	Article (a); Homonyms (one, hours); Com. (before **but** in comp. sentence)
5	Stagecoaches, covered wagons, and a train are included in a mural showing the pioneers' means of travel.	Commas (series); Subj. – v. agree.; Article (a); Apostro. (poss.)
	"We went to the Grand Rapids Art Museum, and we got to sit in a covered wagon," said Nick.	Quot. marks (dir. quot.); Cap. (prop. n. – institution, person); Com. (before **and** in comp. sentence, dir. quot); Verb

1	<u>The Oregon Trail</u>, a book by Francis Parkman, helped Ms. Freeman's class learn about pioneer travel.	Cap. (prop. n. – book, persons, title); Underline (book); Com. (appos.); Period (abbr.); Apostro. (poss.); Verb
	Didn't the discovery of the Cumberland Gap make travel across the Appalachian Mountains easier?	Apostro. (contr.); Cap. (prop. n. – geo. features); Ques. mark
2	"The Cumberland Gap is narrow, and its sides are about five hundred feet high," said Dr. March.	Quot. marks (dir. quot.); Cap. (prop. n. – geo. feature, title, person); Com. (before **and** in comp. sent., dir. quot.); Period (abbr.)
	The pioneers didn't have power tools, so they had to use axes, hammers, and hoes to do their work.	Dbl. subj.; Apostro. (contr.); Subj. – v. agree.; Com. (before **so** in comp. sentence, series); Homonym (their)
3	Independence, Missouri, was the start of the Oregon Trail, and this trail helped expand the United States.	Cap. (prop. n. – city, state, trail, country); Com. (city, state, before **and** in comp. sent.)
	The Sante Fe Trail also began in Independence, Missouri, but it ended in Santa Fe, New Mexico.	Cap. (prop. n. – trail, cities, states); Verb; Com. (cities, states, before **but** in comp. sent.)
4	"Wasn't the Oregon Trail 2,000 miles long?" asked Naomi.	Quot. marks (dir. quot.); Apostro. (contr.); Cap. (prop. n. – trail, person); Com. (number); Ques. mark (dir. quot.)
	The trip took about six months in a covered wagon, and many people died on the trail.	Dbl. subj.; Verb; Com. (before **and** in comp. sent.)
5	What's on Ms. Clark's list of things we need for our play about pioneers traveling west on the trails?	Apostro. (contr., poss.); Cap. (prop. n. – title, person); Period (abbr.); Homonym (for); Ques. mark
	We all thought we needed a spinning wheel, an iron kettle, and a baby's cradle.	Verb; Pron. (case); Com. (series); Art. (an); Apostro. (poss.)

Week 15 – Pioneer Schools

Day			
1	Language Arts	a.	werent parents their childrens teachers in the early pioneer days in the united states
		b.	boys were taught how to hunt farm and use a ax and girls were taught to cook so and weave
2	Science	a.	some of the schools had pens maked from goose quills and there ink was made from berries
		b.	children was needed to work on the farms so they goed to school only two oar three months in the winter
3	Social Studies	a.	aunt marie said the settlers paid there teacher with fruit vegetables and sometimes a live chicken
		b.	what does it mean when the teacher useta get room and board asked ross
4	Math	a.	maggie and ruth they went to a won-room school and one teacher she taught first through eighth grade
		b.	their werent very many children in each grade said grandma post
5	Creative Arts	a.	the teacher and she class putted on a program in may called western hoedown
		b.	wasnt the square dancers fiddle players and singers the best youve ever saw

Week 16 – Famous Pioneers

Day			
1	Language Arts	a.	ronald read life and adventures of daniel boone a book written by michael lofaro
		b.	daniel boone was born on november 2 1734 in a log cabin near the present city of reading pennsylvania
2	Science	a.	did you no that johnny appleseed was a reel man who's name was john chapman
		b.	he planted apple seeds in ohio gived apple seeds and saplings away to people he met and lived to sea thousands of acres of apple orchards in the u s
3	Social Studies	a.	davy crockett was a famous scout hunter humorist and folk hero according to u s history
		b.	davy crockett he were elected to congress when president andrew jackson was inn office
4	Math	a.	in february 1836 davy crockett joined about 185 men to defend the alamo in san antonio texas
		b.	meriwether lewis and william clark led an expedition 7700 miles from st louis missouri to the pacific coast
5	Creative Arts	a.	lets sang the song about davy crockett in our play about famous american pioneers
		b.	will bill rob and ted dress up as kit carson daniel boone and davy crockett asked miss wise

©1993 Instructional Fair, Inc. IF8403 Oral Language

Corrected Sentences  Skills Covered

1	Weren't parents their children's teachers in the early pioneer days in the United States?	Apostro. (contr., poss.); Cap. (prop. n. – country); Ques. mark
	Boys were taught how to hunt, farm, and use an ax, and girls were taught to cook, sew, and weave.	Com. (series, before **and** in comp. sent.); Art. (an); Homonym (sew)
2	Some of the schools had pens made from goose quills, and their ink was made from berries.	Verb; Com. (before **and** in comp. sent.); Homonym (their)
	Children were needed to work on the farms, so they went to school only two or three months in the winter.	Subj. – v. agree.; Com. (before **so** in comp. sent.); Verb; Homonym (or)
3	Aunt Marie said, "The settlers paid their teacher with fruit, vegetables, and sometimes a live chicken."	Cap. (prop. n. – title, person, first word in quot); Com. (dir. quot, series); Quot. marks (dir. quot.); Homonym (their)
	"What does it mean when the teacher used to get room and board?" asked Ross.	Quot. marks (dir. quot.); Enunciation (used to); Ques. mark (dir. quot.); Cap. (prop. n. – person)
4	Maggie and Ruth went to a one-room school, and one teacher taught first through eighth grade.	Cap. (prop. n. – persons); Dbl. subj.; Hom. (one); Com. (before **and** in comp. sent.)
	"There weren't very many children in each grade," said Grandma Post.	Quot. marks (dir. quot.); Homonym (there); Apostro. (contr.); Com. (dir. quot.); Cap. (prop. n. – title, person)
5	The teacher and her class put on a program in May called "Western Hoedown."	Pronoun (case); Verb; Cap. (prop. n. – month, program); Quot. marks (program)
	Weren't the square dancers, fiddle players, and singers the best you've ever seen?	Subj. – v. agree.; Apostro. (contr.); Com. (series); Verb; Ques. mark

1	Ronald read <u>Life and Adventures of Daniel Boone</u>, a book written by Michael Lofaro.	Cap. (prop. n. – persons, book); Underline (book); Com. (appos.)
	Daniel Boone was born on November 2, 1734, in a log cabin near the present city of Reading, Pennsylvania.	Cap. (prop. n. – person, month, city, state); Com. (date, year, city, state)
2	Did you know that Johnny Appleseed was a real man whose name was John Chapman?	Homonyms (know, real, whose); Cap. (prop. n. – persons); Ques. mark
	He planted apple seeds in Ohio, gave apple seeds and saplings away to people he met, and lived to see thousands of acres of apple orchards in the U.S.	Cap. (prop. n. – state, country); Com. (series); Verb; Homonym (see); Periods (abbr.)
3	Davy Crockett was a famous scout, hunter, humorist, and folk hero according to U.S. history.	Cap. (prop. n. – person; prop. adj. – nationality); Com. (series); Periods (abbr.)
	Davy Crockett was elected to Congress when President Andrew Jackson was in office.	Cap. (prop. n. – persons, gov. branch, title); Dbl. subj.; Subj. – v. agree.; Homonym (in)
4	In February, 1836, Davy Crockett joined about 185 men to defend the Alamo in San Antonio, Texas.	Cap. (prop. n. – month, person, historic location, city, state); Com. (month, year, city, state)
	Meriwether Lewis and William Clark led an expedition 7,700 miles from St. Louis, Missouri, to the Pacific coast.	Cap. (prop. n. – persons, city, state; prop. adj. – geo. location); Com. (number, city, state); Period (abbr.)
5	Let's sing the song about Davy Crockett in our play about famous American pioneers.	Apostro. (contr.); Verb; Cap. (prop. n. – person; prop. adj. – nationality)
	"Will Bill, Rob, and Ted dress up as Kit Carson, Daniel Boone, and Davy Crockett?" asked Miss Wise.	Quot. marks (dir. quot.); Cap. (prop. n.– persons, title); Com. (series); Ques. mark (dir. quot.)

Week 17 – Pioneer Homes

Day		
1	Language Arts	a. log cabins were builded buy most pioneers in kentucky tennessee and virginia b. the fireplace were used for cooking but it was the familys favorite gathering place, to
2	Science	a. the pioneers they didnt have nails so they useded wooden pins to hold the parts of the roof together b. the cabins doors were made of wood and the door swung on hinges made of leather said grandpa harper
3	Social Studies	a. a pioneers home were built in only won day at a party called a house-raising said gramma eleanor b. werent the spaces between the logs filled with clay moss or mud
4	Math	a. carl and mr dennis didnt no that sum pioneer families built a half-camp which had a roof and only three sides b. the forth side of a half-camp were open and it faced a fire used to cook food heat water and provide warmth
5	Creative Arts	a. youre quilts pattern was designed by my mother said russ b. pioneer women they maked there quilts from scraps of material thread and birds feathers

Week 18 – Pioneer Food

Day		
1	Language Arts	a. the book frontier living wasnt at mine library so i went to the library on third street b. the book it learned us that corn was the main crop cuz it didnt spoil and could be used in many ways
2	Science	a. how did the pioneers keep there food from spoiling asked cousin nancy b. dad replied sam telled i that they dried their meet in the sun or soaked it in water that was very salty
3	Social Studies	a. a pioneers meal might have ben dear meet grits and wild strawberries b. coffee and tea costed to much so families drank water oar cows milk
4	Math	a. sue had won cup each of sugar flower milk and cornmeal so she could makes johnnycake like the pioneers b. mom asked wont you need sum salt two eggs and won teaspoon of soda, to
5	Creative Arts	a. id goes to greenfield village if you wanna sea lotsa cooking utensils from pioneer days b. didnt the students at westwood school sing jimmy cracked corn in there play on tuesday may 15th

©1993 Instructional Fair, Inc. IF8403 Oral Language

Corrected Sentences  Skills Covered

1	Log cabins were built by most pioneers in Kentucky, Tennessee, and Virginia.	Verb; Homonym (by); Cap. (prop. n. – states); Com. (series)
	The fireplace was used for cooking, but it was the family's favorite gathering place, too.	Subj. – v. agree.; Com. (before **but** in comp. sent.); Apostro. (poss.); Homonym (too)
2	The pioneers didn't have nails, so they used wooden pins to hold the parts of the roof together.	Dbl. subj.; Apostro. (contr.); Com. (before **so** in comp. sent.); Verb
	"The cabin's doors were made of wood, and the door swung on hinges made of leather," said Grandpa Harper.	Quot. marks (dir. quot.); Apostro. (poss.); Com. (before **and** in comp. sent., dir. quot.); Cap. (prop. n. – title, person)
3	"A pioneer's home was built in only one day at a party called a house-raising," said Grandma Eleanor.	Quot. marks (dir. quot.); Apostro. (poss.); Subj. –v. agree.; Hom. (one); Com. (dir. quot.); Cap. (prop. n. – title, person); Enunc. (Grandma)
	Weren't the spaces between the logs filled with clay, moss, or mud?	Apostro. (contr.); Com. (series); Ques. mark
4	Carl and Mr. Dennis didn't know that some pioneer families built a half-camp which had a roof and only three sides.	Cap. (prop. n. – persons, title); Period (abbr.); Apostro. (contr.); Homonyms (know, some)
	The fourth side of a half-camp was open, and it faced a fire used to cook food, heat water, and provide warmth.	Homonym (fourth); Subj. – v. agree.; Com. (before **and** in comp. sent., series)
5	"Your quilt's pattern was designed by my mother," said Russ.	Quot. marks (dir. quot.); Homonym (your); Apostro. (poss.); Com. (dir. quot.); Cap. (prop. n. – person)
	Pioneer women made their quilts from scraps of material, thread, and birds' feathers.	Dbl. subj.; Verb; Homonym (their); Com. (series); Apostro. (poss.)

1	The book <u>Frontier Living</u> wasn't at my library, so I went to the library on Third Street.	Cap. (prop. n. – book, street); Under. (book); Apostro. (contr.); Pronoun (case); Com. (before **so** in comp. sent.)
	The book taught us that corn was the main crop because it didn't spoil and could be used in many ways.	Dbl. subj.; Improper usage (taught); Enunciation (because); Apostro. (contr.)
2	"How did the pioneers keep their food from spoiling?" asked Cousin Nancy.	Quot. marks (dir. quot.); Homonym (their); Ques. mark (dir. quot.); Cap. (prop. n. – title, person)
	Dan replied, "Sam told me that they dried their meat in the sun or soaked it in water that was very salty."	Cap. (persons, first word in quot.) Com. (dir. quot.) Quot. marks (dir. quot.); Verb; Pronoun (case); Homonym (meat)
3	A pioneer's meal might have been deer meat, grits, and wild strawberries.	Apostro. (poss.); Homonyms (been, deer, meat); Com. (series)
	Coffee and tea cost too much, so families drank water or cow's milk.	Verb; Homonyms (too, or); Com. (before **so** in comp. sent.); Apostro. (poss.)
4	Sue had one cup each of sugar, flour, milk, and cornmeal, so she could make johnnycake like the pioneers.	Cap. (prop. n. – person); Homonyms (one, flour); Com. (series, before **so** in comp. sent.); Verb
	Mom asked, "Won't you need some salt, two eggs, and one teaspoon of soda, too?"	Cap. (prop. n. – rel.); Com. (dir. quot., series); Quot. marks (dir. quot.); Apostro. (contr.); Homonyms (some, one, too); Ques. mark (dir. quot.)
5	I'd go to Greenfield Village if you want to see lots of cooking utensils from pioneer days.	Apostro. (contr.); Verb; Cap. (prop. n. – museum); Enunc. (want to, lots of); Homonym (see)
	Didn't the students at Westwood School sing "Jimmy Cracked Corn" in their play on Tuesday, May 15th?	Apostro. (contr.); Cap. (prop. n. – institution, song, day, month); Quot. marks (song); Hom. (their); Com. (day, date); Ques. mark

Week 19 – Balloons

Day			
1	Language Arts	a.	aunt trudy and uncle paul cant wait until they take there hot air balloon ride next sunday at 330 pm
		b.	we taked the same ride in october when all the trees were gorgeous with there red yellow and orange leaves
2	Science	a.	hannah asked i how do the balloons go up in the air
		b.	dr storey told me that the balloons they is filled with gases that are lighter than air
3	Social Studies	a.	the first balloon flight across the english channel were made on january 7 1785 by a french balloonist and an american doctor
		b.	they left from dover england and they landed too hours later near calais france
4	Math	a.	three american balloonists b abruzzo m anderson and l newman made the first atlantic ocean crossing in 1978
		b.	didnt they travel 3233 miles in 137 hours and 6 minutes asked bradley
5	Creative Arts	a.	i thinks of balloons every time me here the song up, up and away
		b.	mine teacher teached us a song about a sheep a rooster and a duck called three in a balloon

Week 20 – Water Transportation

Day			
1	Language Arts	a.	what kinds of vehicles travel in water asked the teacher ms brady
		b.	sandy answered i can only think of boats canoes rafts and submarines
2	Science	a.	ive saw pictures of hydrofoils and hovercraft and i wondered how they was different
		b.	isnt it true that an hovercraft runs on a cushion of air maked buy powerful fans
3	Social Studies	a.	sum factories they use barges to haul coal grain and gravel on the ohio river
		b.	mr harold a tugboat captain has towed many barges but he told us that some barges has there own engines
4	Math	a.	junks chinese wooden sailing vessels has as many as five sails and they can carry heavy loads
		b.	didnt clipper ships in the 1800s sale from new york city to san francisco in three or four months
5	Creative Arts	a.	mrs dawsons class maked a mural of pictures of early american boats
		b.	nancy and brian they drawed there boat going down the mississippi river write in the middle of the mural

©1993 Instructional Fair, Inc.   IF8403 Oral Language

Corrected Sentences    Skills Covered

1	Aunt Trudy and Uncle Paul can't wait until they take their hot air balloon ride next Sunday at 3:30 P.M.	Cap. (prop. n. – titles, persons, day, optional abbr.); Apostro. (contr.); Homonym (their); Colon (time); Periods (abbr.)
	We took the same ride in October when all the trees were gorgeous with their red, yellow, and orange leaves.	Verb; Cap. (prop. n. – mo.); Homonym (their); Com. (series)
2	Hannah asked me, "How do the balloons go up in the air?"	Cap. (prop. n. – person; 1st word of dir. quot.); Pron. (case); Com. (dir. quot.); Quot. marks (dir. quot.); Ques. mark (dir. quot.)
	Dr. Storey told me that the balloons are filled with gases that are lighter than air.	Cap. (prop. n. – title, person); Period (abbr.); Verb.; Dbl. subj.; Subj. – v. agree.
3	The first balloon flight across the English Channel was made on January 7, 1785, by a French balloonist and an American doctor.	Cap. (prop. n. – geographic feature, mo.; prop. adj. – nationalities); Subj. – v. agree.; Com. (date)
	They left from Dover, England, and they landed two hours later near Calais, France.	Cap. (prop. n. – cities, countries); Com. (cities, countries; before **and** in comp. sent.); Hom. (two)
4	Three American balloonists, B. Abruzzo, M. Anderson, and L. Newman, made the first Atlantic Ocean crossing in 1978.	Cap. (prop. adj. – nationality; prop. n. – persons, geographic feature); Com. (appos., series); Periods (abbr.)
	"Didn't they travel 3,233 miles in 137 hours and 6 minutes?" asked Bradley.	Quot. marks (dir. quot.); Apostro. (contr.); Com. (number); Ques. mark (dir. quot.); Cap. (prop. n. – person)
5	I think of balloons every time I hear the song "Up, Up and Away."	Subj. – v. agree.; Pron. (case); Homonym (hear); Cap. (prop. n. – song); Quot. marks (song)
	My teacher taught us a song about a sheep, a rooster, and a duck called "Three in a Balloon."	Pron. (case); Verb; Com. (series); Cap. (prop. n. – song); Quot. marks (song)

1	"What kinds of vehicles travel in water?" asked the teacher, Ms. Brady.	Quot. marks (dir. quot.); Ques. mark (dir. quot.); Com. (appos.); Cap. (prop. n. – title, person); Period (abbr.)
	Sandy answered, "I can only think of boats, canoes, rafts, and submarines."	Cap. (prop. n. – person, 1st word in quot.); Com. (dir. quot., series); Quot. marks (dir. quot.);
2	I've seen pictures of hydrofoils and hovercraft, and I wondered how they were different.	Apostro. (contr.); Verb; Com. (before **and** in comp. sent.); Subj. – v. agree.
	Isn't it true that a hovercraft runs on a cushion of air made by powerful fans?	Apostro. (contr.); Art. (a); Verb; Homonym (by); Ques. mark
3	Some factories use barges to haul coal, grain, and gravel on the Ohio River.	Homonym (some); Dbl. subj.; Com. (series); Cap. (prop. n. – geo. feature)
	Mr. Harold, a tugboat captain, has towed many barges, but he told us that some barges have their own engines.	Cap. (prop. n. – title, person); Period (abbr.); Com. (appos., before **but** in comp. sent.); Subj. – v. agree.; Homonym (their)
4	Junks, Chinese wooden sailing vessels, have as many as five sails, and they can carry heavy loads.	Com. (appos., before **and** in comp. sent.); Cap. (prop. adj. – nationality); Subj. – v. agree.
	Didn't clipper ships in the 1800's sail from New York City to San Francisco in three or four months?	Apostro. (contr., optional date); Homonym (sail); Cap. (prop. n. – cities); Ques. mark
5	Mrs. Dawson's class made a mural of pictures of early American boats.	Cap. (prop. n. – title, person; prop. adj. – nation.); Period (abbr.); Apostro. (poss.); Verb
	Nancy and Brian drew their boat going down the Mississippi River right in the middle of the mural.	Cap. (prop. n. – persons, geo. feature); Dbl. subj.; Verb; Homonyms (their, right)

©1993 Instructional Fair, Inc.   IF8403 Oral Language

Week 21 – Trucks

Day			
1	Language Arts	a.	uncle marvin and mr johnson drived a truck from florida two michigan filled with oranges
		b.	wasnt their a place in the trucks cab to sleep so they could keep driving all night
2	Science	a.	how does trucks help two get fruit vegetables and milk across the united states
		b.	refrigerated trucks keeps fruit and vegetables from spoiling and tanker trucks keeps milk cold
3	Social Studies	a.	all cities towns and villages need garbage trucks too haul away peoples trash mayor bradley explained
		b.	do bart no what kind of truck has ladders hoses and a siren
4	Math	a.	colleen martin cant believe that there is more than 36 million trucks in the united states
		b.	trucks that use interstate highways cant way more than 80000 pounds under us law
5	Creative Arts	a.	jennys picture of she father sitting in his dump truck one first prize at the art show held in september
		b.	miss thomas our art teacher taked the picture to jennys house on saturday

Week 22 – Helicopters

Day			
1	Language Arts	a.	whirlybird eggbeater and chopper they is all names given for an helicopter in mine reading book
		b.	havent you read the book harrys helicopter by joan anderson thats in the oak park library
2	Science	a.	there is lotsa photographs in them books of the inside of volcanoes taked buy scientists from a helicopter
		b.	cant farmers use helicopters to plant seeds fertilize and spray crops asked mr grandy
3	Social Studies	a.	helicopters they has saved many lifes cuz them can get people to an hospital in a hurry
		b.	mercy hospital has a heliport a special pad four helicopters to land on added faith
4	Math	a.	won man using an helicopter can replace 15 to 18 cowhands to rode the range heard the cattle and check fences
		b.	mr smiths men traveled 50 miles to and from there offshore oil rig in the gulf of mexico
5	Creative Arts	a.	us class play called the happy helicopter takes place next wednesday at 200 pm
		b.	do you think nora maria and hank they is having fun twirling around the stage like helicopters

©1993 Instructional Fair, Inc.   IF8403 Oral Language

Corrected Sentences  Skills Covered

1	Uncle Marvin and Mr. Johnson drove a truck from Florida to Michigan filled with oranges.	Cap. (prop. n. – titles, persons, states); Period (abbr.); Verb; Homonym (to)
	Wasn't there a place in the truck's cab to sleep, so they could keep driving all night?	Apostro. (contr., poss.); Homonym (there); Com. (before **so** in comp. sent.); Ques. mark
2	How do trucks help to get fruit, vegetables, and milk across the United States?	Subj. – v. agree.; Homonym (to); Com. (series); Cap. (prop. n. – country); Ques. mark
	Refrigerated trucks keep fruit and vegetables from spoiling, and tanker trucks keep milk cold.	Subj. – v. agree.; Com. (before **and** in comp. sent.)
3	"All cities, towns, and villages need garbage trucks to haul away people's trash," Mayor Bradley explained.	Quot. marks (dir. quot.); Com. (series, dir. quot.); Homonym (to); Apostro. (poss.); Cap. (prop. n. – title, person)
	Does Bart know what kind of truck has ladders, hoses, and a siren?	Subj. – v. agree.; Cap. (prop. n. – person); Homonym (know); Com. (series); Ques. mark
4	Colleen Martin can't believe that there are more than 36 million trucks in the United States.	Cap. (prop. n. – person, country); Apostro. (contr.); Subj. – v. agree.
	Trucks that use interstate highways can't weigh more than 80,000 pounds under U.S. law.	Apostro. (contr.); Homonym (weigh); Com. (number); Cap. (prop. adj. – country); Periods (abbr.)
5	Jenny's picture of her father sitting in his dump truck won first prize at the art show held in September.	Cap. (prop. n. – person, month); Apostro. (poss.); Pronoun (case); Homonym (won)
	Miss Thomas, our art teacher, took the picture to Jenny's house on Saturday.	Cap. (prop. n. – title, persons, day); Com. (appos.); Verb; Apostro. (poss.)

1	Whirlybird, eggbeater, and chopper are all names given for a helicopter in my reading book.	Com. (series); Dbl. subj.; Subj. – v. agree.; Art. (a); Pronoun (case)
	Haven't you read the book <u>Harry's Helicopter</u> by Joan Anderson that's in the Oak Park Library?	Apostro. (contr., poss.); Cap. (prop. n. – book, person, institution); Under. (book); Ques. mark
2	There are a lot of photographs in those books of the inside of volcanoes taken by scientists from a helicopter.	Subj. – v. agree.; Enunciation (a lot of); Dem. adj.; Verb; Homonym (by)
	"Can't farmers use helicopters to plant seeds, fertilize, and spray crops?" asked Mr. Grandy.	Quot. marks (dir. quot.); Apostro. (contr.); Com. (series); Ques. mark (dir. quot.); Cap. (prop. n. – title, person); Period (abbr.)
3	Helicopters have saved many lives because they can get people to a hospital in a hurry.	Dbl. subj.; Subj. – v. agree.; Irreg. plural (lives); Enunciation (because); Pronoun (case); Art. (a)
	"Mercy Hospital has a heliport, a special pad for helicopters to land on," added Faith.	Quot. marks (dir. quot.); Cap. (prop. n. – institution, person); Com. (appos., dir. quot.); Homonym (for)
4	One man, using a helicopter, can replace 15 to 18 cowhands to ride the range, herd the cattle, and check fences.	Homonyms (one, herd); Com. (appos. series); Article (a); Verb
	Mr. Smith's men traveled 50 miles to and from their offshore oil rig in the Gulf of Mexico.	Cap. (prop. n. – title, person, geo. feature); Period (abbr.); Apostro. (poss.); Homonym (their)
5	Our class play called <u>The Happy Helicopter</u> takes place next Wednesday at 2:00 P.M.	Pron. (case); Cap. (prop. n. – play, day, optional abbr.); Underline (play); Colon (time); Periods (abbr.)
	Do you think Nora, Maria, and Hank are having fun twirling around the stage like helicopters?	Cap. (prop. n. – persons); Com. (series); Dbl. subj.; Subj. – v. agree.; Ques. mark

©1993 Instructional Fair, Inc.   25   IF8403 Oral Language

Week 23 – Bicycles

Day		
1	Language Arts	a. doctor ryan telled people at the ford clinic that its healthiest to use muscle power to get around b. us class really used our muscles when we went on a biking trip to greenwood park on friday at 900 am
2	Science	a. my mom wont leave me ride mine bike at night said lonnie b. tamara replied you should has reflectors and lights if you ride you bike at night so cars can see you
3	Social Studies	a. mr po wrote to the bicycle institute of america and they sended he a list of all the u s bicycle clubs b. a bicycle are a very common means of transportation in china said mr ross
4	Math	a. jons report telled us that over nine million bikes were selled in the united states in the early 1980s b. id love to ride a high-wheeler a bicycle with a five-foot front wheel but i bet its to hard
5	Creative Arts	a. park street schools bicycle parade is on the last friday in may and were all getting ready for it b. didnt terry win first prize for her decorated bike asked ms davis

Week 24 – Old Trains

Day		
1	Language Arts	a. our teacher mrs hernandez read us the book little engine that could by watty piper b. cuz their curious martin and corey they started asking she questions about them old trains
2	Science	a. she learned us that regular horses eat hay and oats but iron horses old engines used coal b. tony asked didnt smoke fire and sparks came out of the smokestack as the coal burned two make steam
3	Social Studies	a. peter cooper of baltimore maryland were a pioneer of the steam locomotive in the united states in 1830 b. his engine "Tom Thumb" raced against a horse-drawn car and the engine losted the race cuz it braked down
4	Math	a. the number of locomotives and railroads grew rapidly in the united states after 1830 said grandpa b. over 200 railroad charters had been granted in 11 states by 1835 and over 1000 miles of railroad line has been opened
5	Creative Arts	a. its fun to sing the song ive been working on the railroad b. theres lotsa songs about john henry the african-american railroad worker

©1993 Instructional Fair, Inc. IF8403 Oral Language

Corrected Sentences

Skills Covered

1	Doctor Ryan told people at the Ford Clinic that it's healthiest to use muscle power to get around.	Cap. (prop. n. – title, person, institution); Verb; Apostro. (contr.)
	Our class really used our muscles when we went on a biking trip to Greenwood Park on Friday at 9:00 A.M.	Pronoun (case); Cap. (prop. n. – park, day, optional abbr.); Colon (time); Periods (abbr.)
2	"My mom won't let me ride my bike at night," said Lonnie.	Quot. marks (dir. quot.); Apostro. (contr.); Improper usage (let); Pronoun (case); Com. (dir. quot.); Cap. (prop. n. – person)
	Tamara replied, "You should have reflectors and lights if you ride your bike at night, so cars can see you."	Cap. (prop. n. – person, first word in quot.); Com. (dir. quot., before **so** in comp. sent.); Quot. marks (dir. quot.); Verb; Pronoun (case)
3	Mr. Po wrote to the Bicycle Institute of America, and they sent him a list of all the U.S. bicycle clubs.	Cap. (prop. n. – title, person, organization; prop. adj. – country); Periods (abbr.); Com. (before **and** in comp. sent.); Verb; Pronoun (case)
	"A bicycle is a very common means of transportation in China," said Mr. Ross.	Quot. marks (dir. quot.); Subj. – v. agree.; Cap. (prop. n. – country, title, person); Com. (dir. quot.); Period (abbr.)
4	Jon's report told us that over nine million bikes were sold in the United States in the early 1980's.	Cap. (prop. n. – person, country); Apostro. (poss., optional date); Verbs
	I'd love to ride a high-wheeler, a bicycle with a five-foot front wheel, but I bet it's too hard.	Apostro. (contr.); Com. (appos., before **but** in comp. sent.); Homonym (too)
5	Park Street School's bicycle parade is on the last Friday in May, and we're all getting ready for it.	Cap. (prop. n. – institution, day, month); Apostro. (poss., contr.); Com (before **and** in comp. sent.)
	"Didn't Terry won first prize for her decorated bike?" asked Ms. Davis.	Quot. marks (dir. quot.); Apostro. (contr.); Cap. (prop. n. – persons, title); Ques. mark (dir. quot); Period (abbr.)

1	Our teacher, Mrs. Hernandez, read us the book <u>Little Engine That Could</u> by Watty Piper.	Com. (appos.); Cap. (prop. n. – title, persons, book); Period (abbr.); Under. (book)
	Because they're curious, Martin and Corey started asking her questions about those old trains.	Enunciation (because); Homonym (they're); Com. (intro. phrase); Cap. (prop. n. – persons); Dbl. subj.; Pronoun (case); Dem. adj.
2	She taught us that regular horses eat hay and oats, but iron horses, old engines, used coal.	Improper usage (taught); Com. (before **but** in comp. sent., appos.)
	Tony asked, "Didn't smoke, fire, and sparks come out of the smokestack as the coal burned to make steam?"	Cap. (prop. n. – person, first word in quot.); Com. (dir. quot., series); Quot. marks (dir. quot.); Apostro. (contr.); Verb; Hom. (to); Ques. mark (dir. quot.)
3	Peter Cooper of Baltimore, Maryland, was a pioneer of the steam locomotive in the United States in 1830.	Cap. (prop. n. – person, city, state, country); Com. (city, state); Subj. – v. agree.
	His engine, "Tom Thumb," raced against a horse-drawn car, and the engine lost the race because it broke down.	Com. (appos., before **and** in comp. sent.); Verbs; Enunciation (because)
4	"The number of locomotives and railroads grew rapidly in the United States after 1830," said Grandpa.	Quot. marks (dir. quot.); Cap. (prop. n. – country, person); Com. (dir. quot.)
	Over 200 railroad charters had been granted in 11 states by 1835, and over 1,000 miles of railroad line had been opened.	Com. (before **and** in comp. sent., number); Verb
5	It's fun to sing the song "I've been Working on the Railroad."	Apostro. (contr.); Cap. (prop. n. – song); Quot. marks (song)
	There's a lot of songs about John Henry, the African-American railroad worker.	Apostro. (contr.); Enunc. (a lot of); Cap. (prop. n. – person; prop. adj. – race); Com. (appos.)

Week 25 – Massachusetts

Day			
1	Language Arts	a.	uncle george telled me that their has been four u s presidents who were born in massachusetts
		b.	i thinks that theyre john adams john quincy adams john f kennedy and george bush
2	Science	a.	did you ever here about a lake in massachusetts called lake chaubunagungamaug
		b.	its an indian name and i asked mine teacher if she knowed what it meant
3	Social Studies	a.	the revolutionary war began when the patriots fought the british at lexington and concord on april 19 1775
		b.	did you know that some mans through british tea into boston harbor during the boston tea party
4	Math	a.	the world series in baseball were started in boston in 1903
		b.	josh said the boston team beat the pittsburgh team five games to three
5	Creative Arts	a.	on us trip to massachusetts we tooks pictures of the dancers at the jacob's pillow dance festival
		b.	this festival are held every year in july and august in the city of becket insisted sharon

Week 26 – Montana

Day			
1	Language Arts	a.	ranger walters our guide said that the name montana come from a spanish word meaning mountainous
		b.	larry didnt no that the last chance gulch is the main street of helena the capital city of montana
2	Science	a.	gold were first discovered in the state of montana at grasshopper creek in 1862
		b.	its amazing that copper was finded in an anaconda silver mine exclaimed uncle robert
3	Social Studies	a.	sioux and cheyenne indians wiped out a group of united states cavalrymen serving under gen george a custer
		b.	this battle taked place near the little bighorn river on june 25 1876 and it was known as custers last stand
4	Math	a.	almost 400000000 gallons of water flows daily from the giant springs in the city of great falls montana
		b.	mining account for 31 per cent of the value of all goods produced in montana
5	Creative Arts	a.	mom and dad took us family two the winter carnival in whitefish last february said connie
		b.	didnt they has fun things to dew like skiing skating and sledding

©1993 Instructional Fair, Inc. IF8403 Oral Language

Corrected Sentences  Skills Covered

	Sentence	Skills
1	Uncle George told me that there have been four U. S. Presidents who were born in Massachusetts.	Cap. (prop. n. – titles, person, state; prop. adj. – country); Verb; Homonym (there); Subj. – v. agree.; Periods (abbr.)
	I think that they're John Adams, John Quincy Adams, John F. Kennedy, and George Bush.	Subj. – v. agree.; Apostro. (contr.); Cap. (prop. n. – persons); Com. (series); Period (abbr.)
2	Did you ever hear about a lake in Massachusetts called Lake Chaubunagungamaug?	Homonym (hear); Cap. (prop. n. – state, geo. feature); Ques. mark
	It's an Indian name, and I asked my teacher if she knew what it meant.	Apostro. (contr.); Cap. (prop. adj. – race); Com. (before **and** in compound sentence); Pron. (case); Verb
3	The Revolutionary War began when the patriots fought the British at Lexington and Concord on April 19, 1775.	Cap. (prop. n. – event, nationality, cities, mo.); Com. (date, year)
	Did you know that some men threw British tea into Boston Harbor during the Boston Tea Party?	Irreg. plural (men); Homonym (threw); Cap. (prop. adj. – nationality; prop. n. – geo. feature, event); Ques. mark
4	The World Series in baseball was started in Boston in 1903.	Cap. (prop. n. – event, city); Subj. – v. agreement
	Josh said, "The Boston team beat the Pittsburgh team five games to three."	Cap. (prop. n. – person, 1st word in dir. quot.; prop. adj. – cities); Com. (dir. quot.); Quot. marks (dir. quot.);
5	On our trip to Massachusetts, we took pictures of the dancers at the Jacob's Pillow Dance Festival.	Pronoun (case); Cap. (prop. n. – state, event); Comma (intro. phrase); Verb
	"This festival is held every year in July and August in the city of Becket," insisted Sharon.	Quot. marks (dir. quot.); Subj. – v. agree.; Cap. (prop. n. – months, city, person); Com. (dir. quot.)

	Sentence	Skills
1	Ranger Walters, our guide, said that the name Montana comes from a Spanish word meaning mountainous.	Cap. (prop. n. – title, person, state; prop. adj. – nationality); Com. (appos.); Subj. – v. agree.
	Larry didn't know that the Last Chance Gulch is the main street of Helena, the capital city of Montana.	Cap. (prop. n. – person, street, city, state); Apostro. (contr.); Homonym (know); Com. (appos.)
2	Gold was first discovered in the state of Montana at Grasshopper Creek in 1862.	Subj. – v. agree.; Cap. (prop. n. – state, geo. feature)
	"It's amazing that copper was found in an Anaconda silver mine!" exclaimed Uncle Robert.	Quot. marks (dir. quot.); Apostro. (contr.); Verb; Cap. (prop. n. – city, title, person); Excl. pt. (dir. quot.)
3	Sioux and Cheyenne Indians wiped out a group of United States cavalrymen serving under Gen. George A. Custer.	Cap. (prop. adj. – tribes, nation.; prop. n. – race, title, person); Period (abbr.)
	This battle took place near the Little Bighorn River on June 25, 1876, and it was known as Custer's Last Stand.	Verb; Cap. (prop. n. – geo. feature, month, event); Com. (date, year, before **and** in comp. sent.); Apostro. (poss.)
4	Almost 400,000,000 gallons of water flow daily from the Giant Springs in the city of Great Falls, Montana.	Com. (number, city, state); Subj.-v. agree; Cap. (prop. n. – geo. feature, city, state)
	Mining accounts for 31 per cent of the value of all goods produced in Montana.	Subj. – v. agree.; Cap. (prop. n. – state)
5	"Mom and Dad took our family to the Winter Carnival in Whitefish last February," said Connie.	Quot. marks (dir. quot.); Cap. (prop. n. –rel., event, city, month, person); Pron. (case); Homonym (to); Com. (dir. quot.)
	Didn't they have fun things to do like skiing, skating, and sledding?	Apostro. (contr.); Subj. – v. agree.; Homonym (do); Com. (series); Ques. mark

Week 27 – Missouri

Day			
1	Language Arts	a.	mr reed telled us class that missouris nickname is the show me state
		b.	we herd that, two said greg and harold
2	Science	a.	visitors to the st louis worlds fair in 1904 seen an exhibit of early automobiles
		b.	jill said i read that the first ice-cream cones were maked their when the ice-cream man ran out of dishes
3	Social Studies	a.	the pony express began april 3 1860 and went from st joseph missouri to sacramento california
		b.	it was almost 2000 miles and the riders they maked the trip in about ten days
4	Math	a.	i seen the gateway arch in st louis missouri and its 630 feet tall
		b.	thats something to see but i seen a room in the meramec caverns that are big enough to house 300 automobiles
5	Creative Arts	a.	did you know that mark twain the famous writer was born in florida missouri asked david
		b.	him real name was samuel l clemens and he growed up in hannibal missouri

Week 28 – Minnesota

Day			
1	Language Arts	a.	allan carpenter writed a book called minnesota that mine teacher read to our class
		b.	she learned us many things about this state alice telled aunt joan
2	Science	a.	the science museum of minnesota is in st paul and it contains lotsa exciting exhibits
		b.	the mayo clinic in rochester minnesota was finded by william w mayo and him too sons
3	Social Studies	a.	we seen many gophers on our boy scout trip to minnesota i said to dad
		b.	thats probably why the state is called the gopher state laughed mom
4	Math	a.	miss harris our neighbor didnt no their are more than 10000 lakes in minnesota
		b.	minnehaha falls in minneapolis it is 53 foots high
5	Creative Arts	a.	statues of paul bunyan and him blue ox babe is located in bemidji
		b.	in the play i seen, big ole the blacksmith had to open a new iron mine in minnesota for babes new shoes

©1993 Instructional Fair, Inc.   IF8403 Oral Language

Corrected Sentences  Skills Covered

	Corrected Sentences	Skills Covered
1	Mr. Reed told our class that Missouri's nickname is the "Show Me State."	Cap. (prop. n. – title, person, state, nickname); Period (abbr.); Verb; Pronoun (case); Apostro. (poss.); Quot. marks (nickname)
	"We heard that, too," said Greg and Harold.	Quot. marks (dir. quot.); Homonyms (heard, too); Com. (dir. quot.); Cap. (prop. n. – persons)
2	Visitors to the St. Louis World's Fair in 1804 saw an exhibit of early automobiles.	Cap. (prop. n. – event); Period (abbr.); Apostro. (poss.); Verb
	Jill said, "I read that the first ice-cream cones were made there when the ice-cream man ran out of dishes."	Cap. (prop. n. – person, 1st word in quot.); Com. (dir. quot.); Quot. marks (dir. quot.); Verb; Homonym (there)
3	The pony express began April 3, 1860, and went from St. Joseph, Missouri, to Sacramento, California.	Cap. (prop. n. – month, cities, states); Com. (date, year, cities, states); Period (abbr.)
	It was almost 2,000 miles, and the riders made the trip in about ten days.	Com. (number, before **and** in comp. sent.); Dbl. subj.; Verb
4	I saw the Gateway Arch in St. Louis, Missouri, and it's 630 feet tall.	Verb; Cap. (prop. n. – monument, city, state); Period (abbr.); Com. (city, state, before **and** in comp. sent.); Apostro. (contr.)
	That's something to see, but I saw a room in the Meramec Caverns that is big enough to house 300 automobiles.	Apostro. (contr.); Com. (before **but** in comp. sent.); Verb; Cap. (prop. n. – geo. feature); Subj. – v. agree.
5	"Did you know that Mark Twain, the famous writer, was born in Florida, Missouri?" asked David.	Quot. marks (dir. quot.); Com. (appos., city, state); Cap. (prop. n. – persons, city, state); Ques. mark (dir. quot.)
	His real name was Samuel L. Clemens, and he grew up in Hannibal, Missouri.	Pron. (case); Cap. (prop. n. – person, city, state); Period (abbr.); Com. (before **and** in comp. sent., city, state); Verb

	Corrected Sentences	Skills Covered
1	Allan Carpenter wrote a book called <u>Minnesota</u> that my teacher read to our class.	Cap. (prop. n. – person, book); Verb; Underline (book); Pronoun (case)
	"She taught us many things about this state," Alice told Aunt Joan.	Quot. marks (dir. quot.); Improp. usage (taught); Com. (dir. quot.); Cap. (prop. n. – persons, title); Verb
2	The Science Museum of Minnesota is in St. Paul, and it contains a lot of exciting exhibits.	Cap. (prop. n. – institution, city); Period (abbr.); Com. (before **and** in comp. sent.); Enun. (a lot of)
	The Mayo Clinic in Rochester, Minnesota, was founded by William W. Mayo and his two sons.	Cap. (prop. n. – institution, city, state, person); Com. (city, state); Period (abbr.); Verb; Pron. (case); Hom. (two)
3	"We saw many gophers on our Boy Scout trip to Minnesota," I said to Dad.	Quot. marks (dir. quot.); Verb; Cap. (prop. adj. – organization; prop. n. – state, relationship); Com. (dir. quot.)
	"That's probably why the state is called the "Gopher State," laughed Mom.	Quot. marks (dir. quot., nickname); Apostro. (contr.); Cap. (prop. n. – nickname, relationship); Com. (dir. quot.)
4	Miss Harris, our neighbor, didn't know there are more than 10,000 lakes in Minnesota.	Cap. (prop. n. – title, person, state); Com. (appos., number); Apostro. (contr.); Homonyms (know, there)
	Minnehaha Falls in Minneapolis is 53 feet high.	Cap. (prop. n. – geo. feature, city); Dbl. subj.; Irreg. plural (feet)
5	Statues of Paul Bunyan and his blue ox, Babe, are located in Bemidji.	Cap. (prop. n. – characters, city); Pronoun (case); Com. (appos.); Subj. – v. agree.
	In the play I saw, Big Ole, the blacksmith, had to open a new iron mine in Minnesota for Babe's new shoes.	Verb; Cap. (prop. n. – characters, state); Com. (appos.); Apostro. (poss.)

Week 29 – Maine

Day			
1	Language Arts	a.	a book written by ruth sawyer called the enchanted schoolhouse takes place in lobster cove maine
		b.	the main character brian boru captured a we fairyman and he taked he in a teapot from ireland to maine
2	Science	a.	isnt maine it sometimes called the pine tree state cuz pine trees once maked up many of its forests
		b.	a satellite station which is part of a worldwide communications system are located near andover maine
3	Social Studies	a.	the first democrat elected to the u s senate by maine voters were edmund s muskie
		b.	maines margaret chase smith was the first woman elected to both houses of the u s congress during the 1940s
4	Math	a.	can you believe that about 125 million toothpicks a day are maked in the state of maine asked mrs scott
		b.	sum people like to fish and they try there luck in maines 2500 lakes and ponds and 5000 rivers and streams
5	Creative Arts	a.	theres a house in kennebunk maine that a sea captain named the wedding cake house
		b.	can you guess why him gived the house that name asked charles

Week 30 – Michigan

Day			
1	Language Arts	a.	isnt it easy to find michigan on the united states map asked shawna
		b.	frank agreed that we just hafta look for a state thats shaped like a mitten surrounded buy the great lakes
2	Science	a.	lets look at hour cereal box and see if what we eat for breakfast is maked in battle creek michigan
		b.	battle creek nicknamed the cereal center of the world it produce more breakfast cereal than any other city in the world
3	Social Studies	a.	the gerald r ford museum in grand rapids michigan have many things from the life of that president
		b.	did you know that the carpet sweeper was invented by m r bissell in 1876 in grand rapids
4	Math	a.	what for lakes border the state asked mr rush
		b.	my teacher learned me that they are lake erie lake huron lake michigan and lake superior i answered
5	Creative Arts	a.	the song of hiawatha by henry wadsworth longfellow is a poem that describe the upper peninsula of michigan
		b.	is the state song called michigan, my michigan

©1993 Instructional Fair, Inc. IF8403 Oral Language

Corrected Sentences   Skills Covered

1	A book written by Ruth Sawyer called <u>The Enchanted Schoolhouse</u> takes place in Lobster Cove, Maine.	Cap. (prop. n. – person, book, city, state); Under. (book); Com. (city, state)
	The main character, Brian Boru, captured a wee fairyman, and he took him in a teapot from Ireland to Maine.	Com. (appos., before **and** in comp. sent.); Cap. (prop. n. – character, country, state); Homonym (wee); Verb; Pronoun (case)
2	Isn't Maine sometimes called the "Pine Tree State" because pine trees once made up many of its forests?	Apostro. (contr.); Cap. (prop. n. – state, nickname); Dbl. subj.; Quot. marks (nickname); Enunc. (because); Verb; Ques. mark;
	A satellite station which is part of a worldwide communications system is located near Andover, Maine.	Subj. – v. agree.; Cap. (city, state); Com. (city, state)
3	The first Democrat elected to the U.S. Senate by Maine voters was Edmund S. Muskie.	Cap. (prop. n. – party member, gov. branch, person; prop. adj. – state); Periods (abbr.)
	Maine's Margaret Chase Smith was the first woman elected to both houses of the U.S. Congress during the 1940's.	Cap. (prop. n. – state, person, gov. branch); Apostro. (poss., optional date); Periods (abbr.)
4	"Can you believe that about 125 million toothpicks a day are made in the state of Maine?" asked Mrs. Scott.	Quot. marks (dir. quot.); Verb; Cap. (prop. n. – state, title, person); Ques. mark (dir. quot.); Per. (abbr.)
	Some people like to fish, and they try their luck in Maine's 2,500 lakes and ponds and 5,000 rivers and streams.	Homonyms (some, their); Com. (before **and** in comp. sent., numbers); Cap. (prop. n. – state); Apostro. (poss.)
5	There's a house in Kennebunk, Maine, that a sea captain named the "Wedding Cake House."	Apostro. (contr.); Cap. (prop. n. – city, state, building); Com. (city, state); Quot. marks (nickname)
	"Can you guess why he gave the house that name?" asked Charles.	Quot. marks (dir. quot.); Pronoun (case); Verb; Ques. mark (dir. quot.); Cap. (prop. n. – person)

1	"Isn't it easy to find Michigan on the United States map?" asked Shawna.	Quot. marks (dir. quot.); Apostro. (contr.); Cap. (prop. n. – state, person; prop. adj. – country); Ques. mark (dir. quot.)
	Frank agreed that we just have to look for a state that's shaped like a mitten surrounded by the Great Lakes.	Enunc. (have to); Apostro. (contr.); Homonym (by); Cap. (prop. n. – geo. feature)
2	Let's look at our cereal box and see if what we eat for breakfast is made in Battle Creek, Michigan.	Apostro. (contr.); Homonym (our); Verb; Cap. (prop. n. – city, state); Com. (city, state)
	Battle Creek, nicknamed the "Cereal Center of the World," produces more breakfast cereal than any other city in the world.	Cap. (prop. n. – city, nickname); Com. (appos.); Quot. marks (nickname); Dbl. subj.; Subj. – v. agree.
3	The Gerald R. Ford Museum in Grand Rapids, Michigan, has many things from the life of that President.	Cap. (prop. n. – museum, city, state, title); Period (abbr.); Com. (city, state); Subj. – v. agree.
	Did you know that the carpet sweeper was invented by M.R. Bissell in 1876 in Grand Rapids?	Cap. (prop. n. – person, city); Periods (abbr.); Ques. mark
4	"What four lakes border the state?" asked Mr. Rush.	Quot. marks (dir. quot.); Homonym (four); Ques. mark (dir. quot.); Cap. (prop. n. – title, person); Period (abbr.)
	"My teacher taught me that they are Lake Erie, Lake Huron, Lake Michigan, and Lake Superior," I answered.	Quot. marks (dir. quot.); Improper usage (taught); Cap. (prop. n. – geo. feature); Com. (series, dir. quot.)
5	"The Song of Hiawatha" by Henry Wadsworth Longfellow is a poem that describes the Upper Peninsula of Michigan.	Quot. marks (poem); Cap. (prop. n. – poem, person, geo. location, state); Subj. – v. agree.
	Is the state song called "Michigan, My Michigan"?	Quot. marks (song); Cap. (prop. n. – song); Ques. mark

Week 31 – Yellowstone National Park

Day		

1	Language Arts	dear aunt sally
		    we have seen bears elk and buffaloes in yellowstone national park
		          your niece
		          joan

2	Science	a. yellowstones landscape includes geysers canyons and waterfalls said delores b. wasnt its landscape maked more than 60000 years ago buy erupting volcanoes
3	Social Studies	a. the park it is located mostly in wyoming but sum of it spreads into montana and idaho b. yellowstone was established by the united states congress in 1872 said mr stafford our guide
4	Math	a. old faithful are a geyser inn yellowstone national park and it erupts about every 65 minutes b. i red that 20000 elk live in yellowstone but their are only about 1000 bison
5	Creative Arts	a. josh and him family visited yellowstone and they cent i a postcard of old faithful b. mrs smiths art class painted pictures of swans bald eagles and pelicans after they visited there in august

Week 32 – Rocky Mountain National Park

Day		
1	Language Arts	a. rocky mountain national park was created buy congress in 1915 b. didnt isabella bird wrote a book called a ladys life in the rocky mountains

2	Science	dear grandma and grandpa
		    we seen lotsa animals waterfalls and wildflowers when we visited the rocky mountain national park in colorado
		          love
		          jimmy

3	Social Studies	a. our family went to denver colorado and then wee drived two the rocky mountain national park b. the arapaho indians use to live in the rocky mountains said greg the park ranger
4	Math	a. there are more than 100 peaks over 11000 feet high but do you no the name of the highest peak asked mr len b. longs peak is the highest peak, rising too a height of 14255 feet answered jane
5	Creative Arts	a. uncle art sended i a picture of a wild bear from the rocky mountains b. were going to have juan paint an oil painting of the bear said aunt ruth

Corrected Sentences  Skills Covered

1	Dear Aunt Sally, 　　We have seen bears, elk, and buffaloes in Yellowstone National Park. 　　　　　Your niece, 　　　　　Joan	Cap. (greeting and first word of closing; prop. n. – title, persons, park); Com. (after greeting, series, and closing)
2	"Yellowstone's landscape includes geysers, canyons, and waterfalls," said Delores.	Quot. marks (dir. quot.); Cap. (prop. n. – park, person); Apostro. (poss.); Com. (series, dir. quot.)
	Wasn't its landscape made more than 60,000 years ago by erupting volcanoes?	Apostro. (contr.); Verb; Com. (number); Homonym (by); Ques. mark
3	The park is located mostly in Wyoming, but some of it spreads into Montana and Idaho.	Dbl. subj.; Cap. (prop. n. – states); Com. (before **but** in compound sentence); Homonym (some)
	"Yellowstone was established by the United States Congress in 1872," said Mr. Stafford, our guide.	Quot. marks (dir. quot); Cap. (prop. n. – (park, division of gov., title, person); Com. (dir. quot., appos.); Period (abbr.)
4	Old Faithful is a geyser in Yellowstone National Park, and it erupts about every 65 minutes.	Cap. (prop. n. – geo. feature, park); Subj. – v. agree.; Homonym (in); Com. (before **and** in compound sentence)
	I read that 20,000 elk live in Yellowstone, but there are only about 1,000 bison.	Homonyms (read, there); Com. (numbers, before **but** in comp. sent.); Cap. (prop. – n. park)
5	Josh and his family visited Yellowstone, and they sent me a postcard of Old Faithful.	Cap. (prop. n. – park, geo. feature); Pron. (case); Com. (before **and** in compound sentence); Homonym (sent)
	Mrs. Smith's art class painted pictures of swans, bald eagles, and pelicans after they visited there in August.	Cap. (prop. n. – title, person, month); Period (abbr.); Apostro. (poss.); Com. (series)

1	Rocky Mountain National Park was created by Congress in 1915.	Cap. (prop. n. – park, division of government); Homonym (by)
	Didn't Isabella Bird write a book called <u>A Lady's Life in the Rocky Mountains</u>?	Apostro. (contr., poss.); Cap. (prop. n. – person, book); Verb; Underline (book); Ques. mark
2	Dear Grandma and Grandpa, 　　We saw lots of animals, waterfalls, and wildflowers when we visited the Rocky Mountain National Park in Colorado. 　　　　　Love, 　　　　　Jimmy	Cap. (greeting and first word of closing; prop. n. – park, state, persons); Com. (after greeting, series, and closing); Verb; Enunciation (lots of)
3	Our family went to Denver, Colorado, and then we drove to the Rocky Mountain National Park.	Cap. (prop. n. – city, state, park); Com. (city, state, before **and** in comp. sent.); Homonyms (we, to); Verb
	"The Arapaho Indians used to live in the Rocky Mountains," said Greg, the park ranger.	Quot. marks (dir. quot.); Cap. (prop. n. – tribe, geo. feature, person); Verb; Com. (dir. quot, appos.)
4	"There are more than 100 peaks over 11,000 feet high, but do you know the name of the highest peak?" asked Mr. Len.	Quot. marks (dir. quot.); Com. (num., before **but** in comp. sent.); Hom. (know); Ques. mark (dir. quot.) Cap. (prop. n. – title, pers.); Period (abbr.)
	"Longs Peak is the highest peak, rising to a height of 14,255 feet," answered Jane.	Quot. marks (dir. quot.); Cap. (prop. n. – geo. fea., person); Hom. (to); Com. (num., dir. quot.)
5	Uncle Art sent me a picture of a wild bear from the Rocky Mountains.	Cap. (prop. n. – title, person, geo. feature); Verb; Pron. (case)
	"We're going to have Juan paint an oil painting of the bear," said Aunt Ruth.	Quot. marks (dir. quot.); Apostro. (contr.); Cap. (prop. n. – persons, title); Com. (dir. quot.)

©1993 Instructional Fair, Inc.

Week 33 – Mammoth Cave National Park

Day			
1	Language Arts	a.	mammoth cave national park were established inn 1941 and it attracts about 2000000 visitors each year
		b.	isnt mammoth cave about 100 miles south of louisville kentucky asked becky
2	Science	a.	dr yang said i think the blindfish found in the cave once had eyes which have now disappeared cuz the fish lived in darkness so long
		b.	other blind creatures living in mammoth cave include beetles crayfish and bats said mr earl his assistant
3	Social Studies		dear brad 　　arent you surprised that their was indian moccasins and tools found in the cave in the 1700s 　　　　　　your friend 　　　　　　mike
4	Math	a.	isnt echo river the largest river in mammoth cave
		b.	the echo river in mammoth cave is 20 to 60 feet wide and its 5 to 25 feet deep
5	Creative Arts	a.	the park rangers wouldnt leave us take pictures in sum of the caves so we buyed postcards instead
		b.	us buyed ate cards and wee sended them to friends neighbors and relatives in ohio

Week 34 – Sequoia National Park

Day			
1	Language Arts	a.	sequoia national park was established on september 25 1890 which was 18 years after yellowstone were created
		b.	we read about sequoia national park in our countrys national parks a book by irving robert melbo
2	Science	a.	one of the highest peaks in the united states is mount whitney said mrs williams
		b.	you can see 100 miles to the east from the top of mount whitney cuz its 14495 foots high
3	Social Studies		dear aunt helen 　　i bet you didnt know that sequoia national park was named after sequoya a famous cherokee indian 　　　　　　your nephew 　　　　　　kyle
4	Math	a.	their is over 900 miles of trails in sequoia national park said the park ranger
		b.	did you no that sequoia trees can bee 272 feet high and they often measure more than 10 feet in diameter
5	Creative Arts	a.	one giant sequoia the general sherman tree it are photographed by many people cuz its so big
		b.	mr kings oil painting of mount whitney one first prize in the fremont art show

Corrected Sentences    # Skills Covered

1	Mammoth Cave National Park was established in 1941, and it attracts about 2,000,000 visitors each year.	Cap. (prop. n. – park); Subj. – v. agree.; Homonym (in); Com. (before **and** in comp. sentence, number)
	"Isn't Mammoth Cave about 100 miles south of Louisville, Kentucky?" asked Becky.	Quot. marks (dir. quot.); Apostro. (contr.); Cap. (prop. n. – geo. feature, city, state, person); Com. (city, state); Ques. mark
2	Dr. Yang said, "I think the blindfish found in the cave once had eyes which have now disappeared because the fish lived in darkness so long."	Cap. (prop. n. – title, person, first word in quote.); Period (abbr.); Com. (dir. quot.); Quot. marks (dir. quot.); Enunciation (because)
	"Other blind creatures living in Mammoth Cave include beetles, crayfish, and bats," said Mr. Earl, his assistant.	Quot. marks (dir. quot.); Cap. (prop. n. – geo. feature, title, person); Com. (series, dir. quot., appos.); Period (abbr.)

3	Dear Brad,
	    Aren't you surprised that there were Indian moccasins and tools found in the cave in the 1700's?
	    Your friend,
	    Mike
		Cap. (greeting and first word of closing; prop. n. – persons, race); Com. (after greeting and closing); Apostro. (contr., optional date); Homonym (there); Subj. – v. agree.; Ques. mark

4	Isn't Echo River the largest river in Mammoth Cave?	Apostro. (contr.); Cap. (prop. n. – geo. features); Ques. mark
	The Echo River in Mammoth Cave is 20 to 60 feet wide, and it's 5 to 25 feet deep.	Cap. (prop. n. – geo. features); Com. (before **and** in comp. sent.); Apostro. (contr.)
5	The park rangers wouldn't let us take pictures in some of the caves, so we bought postcards instead.	Apostro. (contr.); Improper usage (let); Homonym (some); Com. (before **so** in comp. sent.); Verb
	We bought eight cards, and we sent them to friends, neighbors, and relatives in Ohio.	Pronoun (case); Verbs; Homonyms (eight, we); Com. (before **and** in comp. sent., series); Cap. (prop. n. – state)

1	Sequoia National Park was established on September 25, 1890, which was 18 years after Yellowstone was created.	Cap. (prop. n. – parks, month); Com. (date, year); Subj. – v. agree.
	We read about Sequoia National Park in <u>Our Country's National Parks</u>, a book by Irving Robert Melbo.	Cap. (prop. n. – park, book, person); Apostro. (poss.); Com. (appos.); Under. (book)
2	"One of the highest peaks in the United States is Mount Whitney," said Mrs. Williams.	Quot. marks (dir. quot.); Cap. (prop. n. –country, geo. feature, title, person); Com. (dir. quot.); Period (abbr.)
	You can see 100 miles to the east from the top of Mount Whitney because it's 14,495 feet high.	Cap. (prop n. – geo. feature); Enunciation (because); Apostro. (contr.); Com. (number); Irreg. plural (feet)

3	Dear Aunt Helen,
	    I bet you didn't know that Sequoia National Park was named after Sequoya, a famous Cherokee Indian.
	    Your nephew,
	    Kyle
		Cap. (greeting and first word of closing; prop. n. – title, persons, park, race; prop. adj. – tribe); Com. (after greeting, appos., closing); Apostro. (contr.)

4	"There are over 900 miles of trails in Sequoia National Park," said the park ranger.	Quot. marks (dir. quot.); Homonym (there); Subj. – v. agree.; Cap. (prop. n. – park); Com. (dir. quot.)
	Did you know that sequoia trees can be 272 feet high, and they often measure more than 10 feet in diameter?	Homonyms (know, be); Com. (before **and** in comp. sent.); Ques. mark
5	One giant sequoia, the General Sherman Tree, is photographed by many people because it's so big.	Com. (appos.); Cap. (prop. n. – thing); Dbl. subj.; Subj. – v. agree.; Enunciation (because); Apostro. (contr.)
	Mr. King's oil painting of Mount Whitney won first prize in the Fremont Art Show.	Cap. (prop. n. – title, person, geo. feature, event); Period (abbr.); Apostro. (poss.); Homonym (won)

©1993 Instructional Fair, Inc.

Week 35 – Grand Canyon National Park

Day		
1	Language Arts	a. we read a book a field guide to the grand canyon by stephen whitney said alice and bobbi b. we wanna drive our knew oldsmobile to northwest arizona next july to see the grand canyon

2	Science	hi charlie
		    i finded granite limestone sandstone and shale rocks near the colorado river
		                  your pal
		                    simon

3	Social Studies	a. isnt grand canyon national park larger than the state of rhode island b. its fun to hike the 400 miles of trails raft down the colorado river and ride mules down into the canyon
4	Math	a. visitors might get dizzy at the top of the canyon cause its about 2793 meters above sea level wear the air is thin b. its about 214 miles along the canyon by rode but its 21 miles if you walk straight threw the canyon
5	Creative Arts	a. the brown and red rocks of the grand canyon photograph beautifully said ms taylor b. lets look in the national geographic magazine to sea there pictures of the grand canyon

Week 36 – Great Smoky Mountains National Park

Day		

1	Language Arts	dear mom and dad
		    our boy scout troop is camping in the great smoky mountains national park until friday may 12th
		                  love
		                  kent

2	Science	a. the great smoky mountains they are called that cause they is often covered by a smoky mist said aunt cathy b. i wonder if the smoky mist are worse in july or august inquired sara
3	Social Studies	a. the great smoky mountains national park it was established in 1930 said mr pohl our teacher b. do you thinks the regions first settlers was pioneers oar the cherokee indians
4	Math	a. arent their about 600 miles of streams witch is full of trout b. we drived seventy miles threw the park on the appalachian national scenic trail and us seen many beautiful sights
5	Creative Arts	a. rita singed for songs at the folk festival of the smokies in september and she danced, to b. someone in the audience ask she two perform at the grand ole opry house in nashville tennessee

Corrected Sentences    # Skills Covered

1	"We read a book, <u>A Field Guild to the Grand Canyon</u>, by Stephen Whitney," said Alice and Bobbi.	Quot. marks (dir. quot.); Com. (appos., dir. quot.); Cap. (prop. n. – book, persons); Under. (book)
	We want to drive our new Oldsmobile to northwest Arizona next July to see the Grand Canyon.	Enunc. (want to); Homonym (new); Cap. (prop. n. – brand name, state, month, geo. feature)

2	Hi Charlie,
	      I found granite, limestone, sandstone, and shale rocks near the Colorado River.
	         Your pal,
	         Simon
		Cap. (greeting and first word of closing; prop. n. – persons, geo. feature); Com.(after greeting, series, and closing); Verb

3	Isn't Grand Canyon National Park larger than the state of Rhode Island?	Apostro. (contr.); Cap. (prop. n. – park, state); Ques. mark
	It's fun to hike the 400 miles of trails, raft down the Colorado River, and ride mules down into the canyon.	Apostro. (contr.); Com. (series); Cap. (prop. n.– geo. feature)
4	Visitors might get dizzy at the top of the canyon because it's about 2,793 meters above sea level where the air is thin.	Enunc. (because); Apostro. (contr.); Com. (number); Homonym (where)
	It's about 214 miles along the canyon by road, but it's 21 miles if you walk straight through the canyon.	Apostro. (contr.); Homonyms (road, through); Com. (before **but** in comp. sent.)
5	"The brown and red rocks of the Grand Canyon photograph beautifully," said Ms. Taylor.	Quot. marks (dir. quot.); Cap. (prop. n. – geo. feature, title, person); Com. (dir. quot.); Period (abbr.)
	Let's look in the <u>National Geographic</u> magazine to see their pictures of the Grand Canyon.	Apostro. (contr.); Cap. (prop. n. – magazine, geo. feature); Under. (magazine); Hom. (see, their)

1	Dear Mom and Dad,
	      Our Boy Scout Troop is camping in the Great Smoky Mountains National Park until Friday, May 12th.
	         Love,
	         Kent
		Cap. (greeting and first word of closing; prop. n. – persons, organization, park, day, month); Com. (after greeting, day, closing)

2	"The Great Smoky Mountains are called that because they are often covered by a smoky mist," said Aunt Cathy.	Quot. marks (dir. quot.); Cap. (prop. n. – geo. feature, title, person); Dbl. subj.; Enunc. (because); Subj. – v. agree.; Com. (dir. quot.)
	"I wonder if the smoky mist is worse in July or August?" inquired Sara.	Quot. marks (dir. quot.); Subj. – v. agree.; Cap. (prop. n. – months, person); Ques. mark (dir. quot.)
3	"The Great Smoky Mountains National Park was established in 1930," said Mr. Pohl, our teacher.	Quot. marks (dir. quot.); Cap. (prop. n. – park, title, person); Dbl. subj.; Com. (dir. quot., appos.); Period (abbr.)
	Do you think the region's first settlers were pioneers or the Cherokee Indians?	Verb; Apostro. (poss.); Subj. – v. agree.; Homonym (or); Cap. (prop. n. – tribe); Ques. mark
4	Aren't there about 600 miles of streams which are full of trout?	Apostro. (contr.); Homonyms (there, which); Subj. – v. agree.; Ques. mark
	We drove seventy miles through the park on the Appalachian National Scenic Trail, and we saw many beautiful sights.	Verbs; Hom. (through); Cap. (prop. n. – trail); Com. (before **and** in comp. sent.); Pronoun (case)
5	Rita sang four songs at the Folk Festival of the Smokies in September, and she danced, too.	Verb; Homonyms (four, too); Cap. (prop. n. – event, month); Com. (before **and** in comp. sent.)
	Someone in the audience asked her to perform at the Grand Ole Opry House in Nashville, Tennessee.	Verb; Pronoun (case); Homonym (to); Cap. (prop. n. – building, city, state); Com. (city, state)

©1993 Instructional Fair, Inc.   IF8403 Oral Language

Corrected Sentences

Skills Covered

	Corrected Sentences	Skills Covered
1	"We read a book, <u>A Field Guild to the Grand Canyon</u>, by Stephen Whitney," said Alice and Bobbi.	Quot. marks (dir. quot.); Com. (appos., dir. quot.); Cap. (prop. n. – book, persons); Under. (book)
	We want to drive our new Oldsmobile to northwest Arizona next July to see the Grand Canyon.	Enunc. (want to); Homonym (new); Cap. (prop. n. – brand name, state, month, geo. feature)

2	Hi Charlie,
	    I found granite, limestone, sandstone, and shale rocks near the Colorado River.
	        Your pal,
	        Simon
		Cap. (greeting and first word of closing; prop. n. – persons, geo. feature); Com.(after greeting, series, and closing); Verb

3	Isn't Grand Canyon National Park larger than the state of Rhode Island?	Apostro. (contr.); Cap. (prop. n. – park, state); Ques. mark
	It's fun to hike the 400 miles of trails, raft down the Colorado River, and ride mules down into the canyon.	Apostro. (contr.); Com. (series); Cap. (prop. n.– geo. feature)
4	Visitors might get dizzy at the top of the canyon because it's about 2,793 meters above sea level where the air is thin.	Enunc. (because); Apostro. (contr.); Com. (number); Homonym (where)
	It's about 214 miles along the canyon by road, but it's 21 miles if you walk straight through the canyon.	Apostro. (contr.); Homonyms (road, through); Com. (before **but** in comp. sent.)
5	"The brown and red rocks of the Grand Canyon photograph beautifully," said Ms. Taylor.	Quot. marks (dir. quot.); Cap. (prop. n. – geo. feature, title, person); Com. (dir. quot.); Period (abbr.)
	Let's look in the <u>National Geographic</u> magazine to see their pictures of the Grand Canyon.	Apostro. (contr.); Cap. (prop. n. – magazine, geo. feature); Under. (magazine); Hom. (see, their)

	Corrected Sentences	Skills Covered

1	Dear Mom and Dad,
	    Our Boy Scout Troop is camping in the Great Smoky Mountains National Park until Friday, May 12th.
	        Love,
	        Kent
		Cap. (greeting and first word of closing; prop. n. – persons, organization, park, day, month); Com. (after greeting, day, closing)

2	"The Great Smoky Mountains are called that because they are often covered by a smoky mist," said Aunt Cathy.	Quot. marks (dir. quot.); Cap. (prop. n. – geo. feature, title, person); Dbl. subj.; Enunc. (because); Subj. – v. agree.; Com. (dir. quot.)
	"I wonder if the smoky mist is worse in July or August?" inquired Sara.	Quot. marks (dir. quot.); Subj. – v. agree.; Cap. (prop. n. – months, person); Ques. mark (dir. quot.)
3	"The Great Smoky Mountains National Park was established in 1930," said Mr. Pohl, our teacher.	Quot. marks (dir. quot.); Cap. (prop. n. – park, title, person); Dbl. subj.; Com. (dir. quot., appos.); Period (abbr.)
	Do you think the region's first settlers were pioneers or the Cherokee Indians?	Verb; Apostro. (poss.); Subj. – v. agree.; Homonym (or); Cap. (prop. n. – tribe); Ques. mark
4	Aren't there about 600 miles of streams which are full of trout?	Apostro. (contr.); Homonyms (there, which); Subj. – v. agree.; Ques. mark
	We drove seventy miles through the park on the Appalachian National Scenic Trail, and we saw many beautiful sights.	Verbs; Hom. (through); Cap. (prop. n. – trail); Com. (before **and** in comp. sent.); Pronoun (case)
5	Rita sang four songs at the Folk Festival of the Smokies in September, and she danced, too.	Verb; Homonyms (four, too); Cap. (prop. n. – event, month); Com. (before **and** in comp. sent.)
	Someone in the audience asked her to perform at the Grand Ole Opry House in Nashville, Tennessee.	Verb; Pronoun (case); Homonym (to); Cap. (prop. n. – building, city, state); Com. (city, state)

©1993 Instructional Fair, Inc.   IF8403 Oral Language